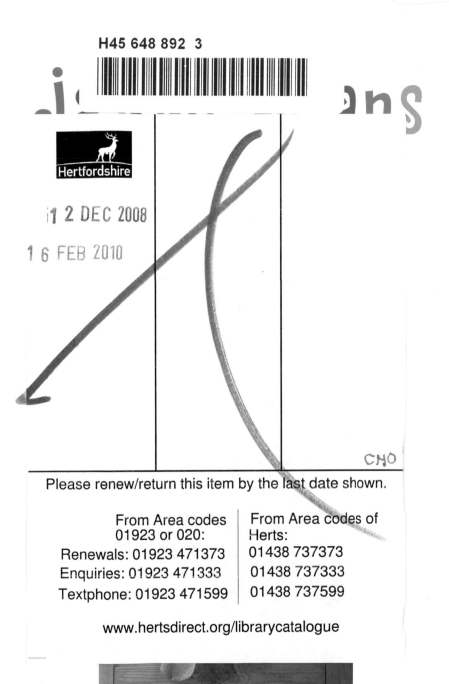

Jazzy Jeans

Mickey Baskett

STERLING

New York / London
www.sterlingpublishing.com

Prolific Impressions Production Staff:

Editor in Chief: Mickey Baskett
Copy Editor: Phyllis Mueller
Graphics: Dianne Miller, Karen Turpin
Styling: Lenos Key
Photography: Jerry Mucklow
Administration: Jim Baskett

Every effort has been made to insure that the information presented is accurate. Since we have no control over physical conditions, individual skills, or chosen tools and products, the publisher disclaims any liability for injuries, losses, untoward results, or any other damages which may result from the use of the information in this book. Thoroughly read the instructions for all products used to complete the projects in this book, paying particular attention to all cautions and warnings shown for that product to ensure their proper and safe use.

STERLING and the distinctive Sterling logo are registered trademarks of Sterling Publishing Co., Inc.

Library of Congress Cataloging-in-Publication Data Available

10 9 8 7 6 5 4 3 2 1

Published by Sterling Publishing Co., Inc.
387 Park Avenue South, New York, NY 10016
© 2006 by Prolific Impressions, Inc.
Distributed in Canada by Sterling Publishing
c/o Canadian Manda Group, 165 Dufferin Street,
Toronto, Ontario, Canada M6K 3H6
Distributed in the United Kingdom by GMC Distribution Services,
Castle Place, 166 High Street, Lewes, East Sussex, England BN7 1XU
Distributed in Australia by Capricorn Link (Australia) Pty. Ltd.
P.O. Box 704, Windsor, NSW 2756, Australia

Printed in China
All rights reserved

Sterling ISBN 978-1-4027-3513-4 (hardcover)

Sterling ISBN 978-1-4027-6272-7 (paperback)

For information about custom editions, special sales, premium and corporate purchases, please contact Sterling Special Sales Department at 800-805-5489 or specialsales@sterlingpublishing.com.

Acknowledgements

A special thank you to the following manufacturers for supplying products for use in creating the projects in this book:

Abby Riba from the Kandi Corporation for creating jeans projects using Zwade® fusible suede and Swarovski® crystals applied with the Kandi Kane™ tool.

Creative Crystal Company, (www.creative-crystal.com) for the BeJeweler™ Tool and Swarovski® crystals

Kandi Corporation, (www.kandicorp.com) for the Kandi Kane™ tool that applies hot fix crystals and gems; Zwade™ fusible suede; and Crystal Shimmer Sheets.

Plaid Enterprises, Inc., (www.plaidonline.com) for supplying sequin and stud iron-on designs, as well as embroidered iron-on designs from their *Jean-e-ology* line of denim iron-on embellishments.

Walnut Hollow Corporation, (www.walnuthollow.com) for the Creative Textile Tool for applying hot fix items.

Contents

Jeans are everywhere. In cities, in the suburbs, in the country, in every season. On grandmas and working women, on soccer moms and movie stars, on teens, and kids, and babies. Jeans are a symbol of casual chic in restaurants and night spots, on campus and in the classroom, at the office and on the factory floor, in the garden and on the playground. We're awash in a sea of denim blue.

Jazzing Up Your Jeans

Think of your jeans as an artist would approach a blank canvas. Because they are so basic and so universally available, jeans lend themselves beautifully to embellishing and personalizing. That's what this book is about. In these pages, you'll see a wealth of ideas for distressing jeans with a variety of tools and techniques. You'll learn easy ways to use appliques, studs, beads, and stones to create one-of-a-kind looks. You can explore hand-embroidered embellishments like leather monograms and shisha-style framed sequins, machine-embroidered appliques and designs on fusible suede, and colorful painted looks for jeans, jackets, and purses.

In addition to all the jeans we're wearing, there are the jeans we're not wearing, at least not right now. These are the jeans the kids have outgrown, the ones with the stain that won't come out, the ones that no longer fit the way you wish they did, the ones that don't seem as stylish as they once were. Possibly these jeans are sentimental favorites as well, ones we

can't quite let go of because they hold treasured memories.

All of these jeans are candidates for transformation, and the last part of this book addresses "Jeans Makeovers." You'll find lots of ideas – wearables such as a swirl skirt and home decor items like cabbage rose pillows and a pocketed organizer. There are useful totes and bags and purses galore, including a diaper duffle bag, plus two ideas for stylish aprons, a fun tooth fairy pillow, and a journal with denim covers and pages made from handmade denim paper.

Make them as we did, or use them as a departure point for your own ideas and artistry. We've included sections on supplies and techniques, and each project includes instructions with photographs, patterns, and diagrams that tell the story of how we did each one, step-by-step. Enjoy them all.

Mickey Baskett

7

About Denim

Denim is a durable woven twill fabric traditionally made from cotton that is now also made from blends of cotton and polyester or other synthetics, with or without the addition of stretchable fibers. It comes in a variety of weights, colors, and finishes. Denim is used for casual clothing, such as jeans, skirts, jackets, shorts, and children's clothes and for protective clothing. Lighter weight denims are used for dresses; less casual clothes may contain more polyester.

The twill weave is one of the three basic weaves (the others are plain and satin). Twill weaves are used to produce fabric that is strong, durable, and firm. Twill fabrics are characterized by a diagonal rib (the twill). When the ribs run upward from left to right, it's called a right hand twill. A left hand twill – the traditional denim weave – has the diagonal rib running upward from right to left. Left hand twills are softer and not as durable; right-hand twills are more rugged.

Most denims are yarn-dyed twills, meaning the yarn is dyed before it is woven. Usually, the warp yarns are colored and the fill (weft) yarns are white.

The weight of the fabric is determined by weighing one yard of fabric. Some popular denim weights are 5 oz., 7 oz., 9.5 oz., 10 oz., 11.5 oz., 12 oz., and 14.5 oz. Jeans are typically made of heavier-weight denim. Heavier denims may be stiff and unyielding when new, but they soften with washing and wear. Strong and hard-wearing, denim fades to whitish patches at creases or points of strain, hem

Twill weave

8

edges, etc., and creases easily.

Traditionally, denim is blue and indigo-dyed. A popular theory about the origins of the word "denim" is that it is derived from *serge de Nimes*, a twill fabric woven in France in the 17th and 18th centuries. At about this time a fabric called "jeans" was being woven in Genoa, Italy and was used to make trousers for sailors. The French *bleu de Genes*, from the Italian *blu di genova* (literally the "blue of Genoa") referred to the color of the fabric and is believed to be the root of the name "blue jeans."

Levi Strauss, a Bavarian immigrant dry goods merchant who moved from New York to San Francisco during the California Gold Rush in 1853, is credited with creating the blue jean as we know it today. His "waist overalls," first worn by miners and railroad workers, were a wardrobe staple of working people and his name became synonymous with the sturdy five-pocketed, riveted denim pants that are an American classic. Adopted by college students in the 1960s and now mass produced in a variety of styles and price ranges, jeans enjoy continued popularity.

Transferring Patterns

Here's an easy method for transferring patterns to denim. You'll need tracing paper, a pencil, bridal tulle fabric, a fine-tip permanent marker, and light-colored chalk.

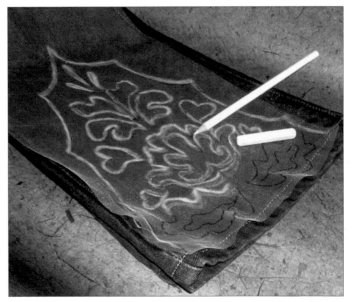

Trace the pattern: Trace the pattern from the book onto tracing paper using a pencil. If needed, enlarge on a photocopier to desired size. Place a piece of bridal tulle over the pattern and retrace the pattern onto the tulle with a permanent marker.

Transfer the pattern: Position the tulle pattern over the denim. Go over the pattern lines with white chalk (for temporary lines) or a fine-tip permanent marker (for permanent lines). Remove tulle and your pattern will be transferred to surface.

Distressing Denim

Most of us prefer jeans and other denim garments that exhibit the characteristics of age and wear – garments that look comfortably broken in and not new. This section shows you various techniques for giving denim the look of wear by removing color by washing, bleaching, and using tools to abrade the surface.

Cutting & Washing

An easy way to distress your jeans is to cut them, then wash them. The cut edges will fray slightly and create a fringe-like edging. You can cut holes or shapes in your jeans and after washing, the holes will look like they have been worn into the jeans. You could also cut slits for the same effect.

This photo shows a shape cut into the jeans. Scissors were used to do the cutting.

A fun look is to cut a shape, such as a star, heart, etc. Then wash the jeans. Then you can sew or fuse a piece of fabric behind the cut out shape for an interesting patch. Each time the jeans are washed the edges will continue to fray slightly. If you wish to prevent further fraying, machine topstitch the jeans just outside the opening.

This photo shows the cut shape after one washing. The edges have frayed into a fringe-like look.

Color Removal

There are a variety of ways to remove color from denim to make it look worn and aged.
You can also use color removal to create designs.

The jacket as purchased.

WASHING

Over time and many washings, denim will fade. This series of photos shows the results of using various combinations of laundry products and washing machine options to produce quicker fading, using a new jeans jacket as an example. All were washed and rinsed, then machine dried.

Treated with powdered color remover: 1 box color remover in washing machine (hot water, small load/heavily soiled setting). Color remover is sold with dyes in grocery stores.

Washed with borax and chlorine bleach: 1 cup borax, 3 cups bleach, 1/4 cup laundry detergent in washing machine (hot water, small load/heavily soiled setting).

Washed with borax, chlorine bleach, and oxygen bleach: 1 cup borax, 3 cups chlorine bleach, 5/8 cup oxygen bleach in washing machine (alternating agitating and soaking for 2 hours).

Best Method – Washed with chlorine bleach and laundry detergent: 3/4 gallon bleach, 1/2 cup laundry detergent in washing machine (warm water, medium load/heavily soiled setting, alternating agitating and soaking for 1 hour).

USING A BLEACH PEN

A bleach pen – the kind you can buy in grocery stores, intended for removing spots and stains in laundry – can be used to create designs and remove color from jeans. The pen contains a bleaching gel and you can use it to write or draw designs. The effect achieved depends on the length of time the gel stays in contact with the fabric. Placing the treated item in sunlight can enhance the bleaching process.

The photo below shows seven examples. The captions tell you how long the bleaching gel was on the fabric before it was washed out.

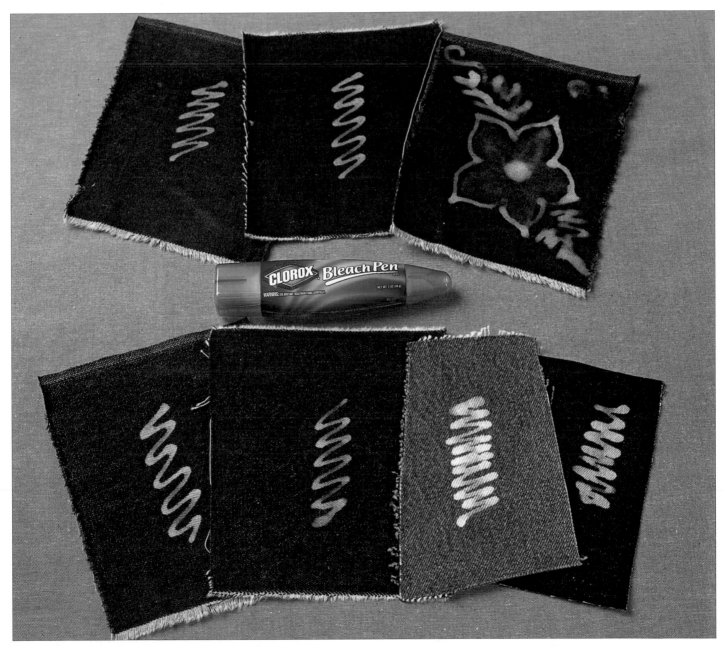

Left to right, top row: 1 hour, 2 hours, 2-1/2 hours
Left to right, bottom row: 3 hours, 24 hours, 1 week on faded denim, 1 week on new denim

Cookie Cutter Distressing

You can use metal or plastic cookie cutters to create distressed designs on pockets or other areas. Simply place the cookie cutter under the fabric or inside the pocket and rub with a fine metal file or sandpaper to reveal the design. Stop when the result pleases you.

With a metal cookie cutter on dry fabric: A metal cookie cutter was placed inside a dry denim pocket and rubbed with a fine metal file and sandpaper.

With a plastic cookie cutter on dampened fabric: A plastic cookie cutter was placed inside a pocket that had been moistened with water (fabric softener can also be used) and was rubbed with sandpaper and fine metal file.

Sandpaper Distressing

You can remove color from an area of denim by rubbing with fine sandpaper on the dry surface.

The area where the label was removed from these jeans isn't faded.

Rubbing sandpaper over the area removes the surface color.

Metal File Distressing

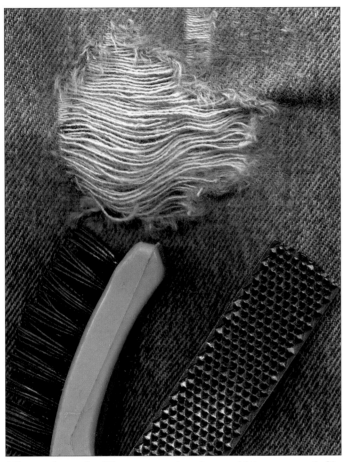

Most denim is yarn-dyed, with white thread in one direction and blue thread in the other. You can create the look of age and wear by removing some of the top (blue) threads from jeans. The white (lower) threads will hold the fabric together. Using a metal file gives you more control than using a steel brush on a drill. (More about this on the following page.)

Step 1: Begin by rubbing the file across the jeans fabric. The file cuts the blue threads.

The end result. The process involves rubbing a metal file horizontally across the jeans fabric. Again using a horizontal motion, brush away the lint that accumulates with a stiff-bristle brush.

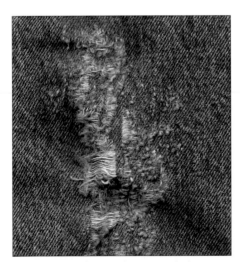

Step 2: Brush in a horizontal direction with a stiff brush to remove the blue fibers.

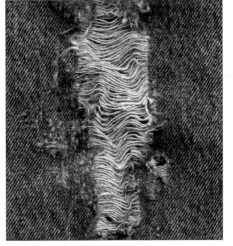

Step 3: Continue to brush until the desired effect is achieved.

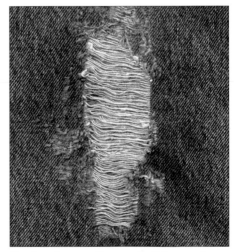

Optional step: Iron a fusible patch on the inside of the jeans under the distressed area.

Steel Brush Distressing

For quick results or to distress large areas, use a high-speed multi-purpose rotary tool with a steel brush attachment or an electric drill with a steel brush to remove surface fibers. Use the tool to remove fibers from areas that would naturally wear over time, such as the edges of pockets, hems, or the upper front areas of legs.

Before: A jeans pocket before distressing.

For heavy distressing: Use a steel brush attachment on an electric drill. The fibers – blue ones and white ones – rip quickly with this method.

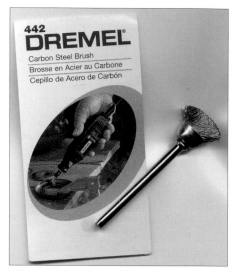

The steel brush attachment for a multi-purpose tool.

For lighter distressing: Use a steel brush attachment on a high-speed multi-purpose tool. It quickly removes surface fibers, but offers more control than an electric drill.

The steel brush on a multi-purpose tool used to lightly distress a jeans leg.

BLEACHED BATIK JEANS
Instructions appear on page 18.

Bleach Pen Batik Jeans

The look of batik, the wax-resist dyeing technique that originated in Asia, is the inspiration for these jeans. The term batik originates from the Malay word for dot or point ("titik") and the Javanese word that means "to write" ("amba"). Batik fabrics are made by applying melted wax to fabric before it is dyed; the waxed areas don't take the dye. Our technique uses a bleach pen to remove color and outline a design. Pearlescent paints are added for color.

Designed by Patty Cox

Pictured on page 17

SUPPLIES

Jeans

Bleach pen

Acrylic pearl paints:

Magenta

Plum

Purple

Green

Teal

Dark blue

Textile medium

5mm iridescent sequins

Clear seed beads

Beading thread

Sewing thread

TOOLS

Beading needle

Scissors

Sewing machine

INSTRUCTIONS

Cutting & Fringing:

Cut jeans to desired length. Create fringe, using one of the following methods:

Method 1:

1. Pull away threads from the cut edges. (Photo 1)
2. Using a sewing machine, straight stitch 1/2" from the cut edge to keep jeans from fraying further.

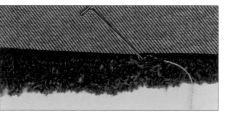

Photo 1 – Threads removed from the bottom of jeans legs to make fringe.

Photo 2 – Threads removed from denim strip to make fringe.

Photo 3 – Fringe sewn to bottom of jeans legs.

Method 2:

Note: Many jeans are not cut on the straight of the grain, and the frayed edges will not be even if you try to fray them by pulling away threads. And sometimes the fringe will be blue

Photo 4 – The design before painting.

threads, not white. To guarantee even, white fringe, use this method.

1. Tear denim strips about 3/4" wide from another pair of jeans.
2. Pull away threads to create fringe on one long edge. (Photo 2)

18

3. With right sides facing and fringe facing up, sew denim strip along hem edges of jeans, using 1/4" seams. Turn down strip. Press. Topstitch 1/8" from seam. (photo 3)

Outlining:

1. Trace pattern and transfer to jeans, using the project photo as a guide for placement. (See "Transferring Patterns" for instructions.) Use the full design on each leg and two smaller flowers and one long leaf just below the pocket on the upper left leg.

2. Go over the transferred design with a bleach pen. (Photo 4) Allow the bleach gel to set one to two hours. Note: Sunlight aids in whitening the design.

3. Wash and dry the jeans.

Painting Inside the White Lines:

1. Mix each paint color with textile medium, following the instructions on the textile medium label.

2. Paint the flowers with magenta. Shade with plum and purple.

3. Paint one side of each leaf with green. Shade with teal.

4. Paint the other side of each leaf with teal. Shade with dark blue. Let dry.

Sequins & Beads:

Stitch sequins and beads randomly around each floral design.

1. Thread the beading needle with thread. Knot one end. Bring needle up from inside of jeans. Add a sequin, then a seed bead. Bring needle around seed bead, then back through sequin to inside of jeans. Knot thread.

2. Repeat for each bead and sequin. ❑

Pattern for Bleach
Pen Batik Jeans
Actual Size

Black Metallica Jeans

Motifs cut from black metallic lace randomly decorate these distressed jeans. Black metallic ribbon covers one side seam and is gathered to make ruffles at the tops of the back pockets. One back pocket sports a distressed star; the other has a heart-shaped lace inset.

Designed by Patty Cox

SUPPLIES

Jeans
2 yds. black metallic ribbon
Black metallic lace motifs
Permanent (washable) fabric glue
Black sewing thread

TOOLS

Multi-purpose high-speed tool with wire cup brush
Metal file
Stiff-bristle brush
Sewing needle
Scissors
Cookie cutters:
　Star-shaped metal
　Heart shape
Fine metal file
Sandpaper
Optional: Sewing machine

INSTRUCTIONS

Legs:
1. Distress jeans as desired, following the instructions at the beginning of this section.
2. Sew the metallic ribbon over the side seam along one leg.
3. Cut floral motifs from lace. Glue in position with fabric glue.
4. When glue dries, whipstitch edges of motifs using needle and thread.

Back Pocket with Star:
Use a star-shaped cookie cutter to make a distressed star on the right back pocket. See "Cookie Cutter Distressing" for instructions.

Back Pocket with Heart:
Make a lace heart-shaped inset for the left back pocket. Here are two options:
Frayed-Edge Heart:
1. Position the heart-shaped cookie cutter on the pocket and trace around it.
2. Carefully cut away the heart shape.
3. Cut a piece of lace larger than the cutout.
4. Insert the lace panel in the pocket. Apply fabric glue under the edges of the heart. Allow glue to dry. Slip a piece of plastic or plastic-covered cardboard into the pocket, under glued area to keep it from getting stuck shut until glue is dry.

Finished-Edge Heart:
1. Remove pocket from jeans.
2. Position the heart-shaped cookie cutter on the pocket and trace around it.
3. Cut out the heart shape.
4. Cut a piece of lace larger than the cutout.
5. Place the lace panel under the cutout in the pocket.
6. Use a sewing machine to stain stitch (applique) around the edge of the heart.
7. Sew the pocket back on the jeans.

Back Pocket Ruffles:
1. Cut two 9" lengths of black metallic ribbon. Gather each along one edge to make a ribbon ruffle as long as the top of the pocket is wide (approximately 6"). Tie off threads to secure gathers.
2. Position the gathered edge of the ribbon inside the top of the pocket. Sew the gathered ribbon to the top of the pocket. ❑

Distressed Stars Jeans

Use a cookie cutter to give your jeans the star treatment. This look can be achieved by either the "Cookie Cutter Distressing" as explained on page 14 and in the instructions that follow; or by using the "Cut & Washed" method as explained on page 11.

Designed by Patty Cox

SUPPLIES

Jeans

Dark denim scraps

1-1/4 yds. gold metallic cording

Light blue sewing thread

Fabric glue

TOOLS

Metal file

Stiff brush

Sandpaper

Star-shaped metal cookie cutter

Sewing machine

Sewing needle

Scissors

INSTRUCTIONS

Distressing:

1. Distress jeans randomly as desired, following the instructions at the beginning of this section.
2. To create the distressed star outlines, place the metal star-shaped cookie cutter inside the jeans. Wrap denim tightly around cookie cutter and hold wrapped denim with one hand while distressing the denim with the other hand. *For a white star outline,* rub over the cookie cutter with sandpaper or the fine edge of a metal file. *For a torn and frayed star outline,* use the rough edge of a metal file.

Pictured above: A distressed outline. A cookie cutter was placed inside the pocket and rubbed with a metal file.

Pictured at left: A frayed edge star cutout reveals a darker denim patch.

Star Cutouts:

1. To make the star cutouts, cut away the fabric inside one or more distressed stars on each leg.
2. Cut a piece of dark denim slightly larger than the cutout and place under the cutout star. Tack in position with fabric glue. Let dry.
3. Set sewing machine to 8 stitches per inch. Machine zig-zag around the edges of the star.
4. Using a stiff brush, rub the denim edges to encourage fraying.

Gold Trim:

Hand or machine stitch gold cording along one leg seam. ❑

Distressed Lacy Jeans

Lace-trimmed pockets and lace cutouts used as appliques give a feminine look to these jeans, which have a distressed area accented with pink embroidery thread.

Designed by Patty Cox

SUPPLIES

Jeans

1/2 yd. lace panel with large motifs

1/2 yd. ecru lace, 1" wide

Permanent fabric glue

Pink embroidery floss

White iron-on patch

Pink sewing thread

TOOLS

Iron

Small scissors

Embroidery needle

Sewing machine

Tools for distressing (See the beginning of this section.)

INSTRUCTIONS

Distressing & Thread Accent:

1. Distress jeans randomly as desired, following the instructions at the beginning of this section. Following the instructions for Metal File Distressing, remove the top threads from a small area on the upper left leg.

2. To make the embroidery thread accent, apply a white iron-on patch on the inside of the jeans under the distressed area on the upper left leg. To add color to the distressed area, sew horizontal stitches through patch, using three strands of embroidery floss. (Photo 1)

Lace Appliques:

1. Cut out several motifs from the lace panel.

Photo 1 – The embroidery thread accent.

Photo 2 – The pocket removed and the lace motif cut out from the panel.

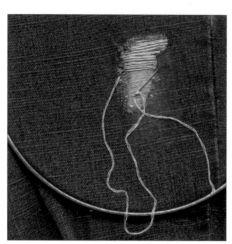

Photo 3 – Lace basted in place; denim behind lace cut away from the back of the pocket.

2. Remove one back pocket. (Photo 2) Hand or machine baste one lace motif on the right side of the pocket.

3. Using small scissors, cut away the denim from the pocket inside the basting stitches. (Photo 3)

Photo 4 – Satin stitching around the lace applique on the front of the pocket.

4. Machine satin stitch around the edges of the motif. (Photo 4)

5. Pin pocket back in position on back of jeans. Machine stitch pocket to jeans.

6. Use remaining lace cutouts to decorate jeans. Apply fabric glue to the back of one motif and glue to the jeans on the outside bottom of the right leg. Choose a small motif and glue on the other back pocket. Add other motifs as desired. Allow glue to dry.
7. Whip stitch the edges of the lace motifs, using a needle and thread.

Front Pocket Trim:
1. For each pocket, cut 9" of ecru lace.
2. Gather lace along bottom edge by hand or machine. Pull threads to gather and tie off threads to secure.
3. Place 1/4" of the gathered edge of the lace inside the top edge of one front pocket. Hand sew lace along the top of the pocket.
4. Repeat steps 2 and 3 to trim the other front pocket. ❑

Applique

Appliques are a fast and easy way to add colorful accents to jeans. In this section, you'll find ideas for using purchased appliques and appliques you make yourself, such as embroidered and jeweled accents and fabric and lace cutouts.

Appliques you can buy include embroidered motifs with a hand-sewn look, stud and rhinestone iron-ons that provide three-dimensional metallic and jewel accents, flocked iron-on appliques that have a velvety texture, and color transfer iron-ons with a handpainted look and feel.

An easy way to attach appliques without iron-on adhesive is to apply a washable permanent fabric glue (sometimes called a "fabric bond") to the back of the applique, position it, and allow to dry. Appliques also can be sewn in place by hand or machine, or adhered with fusible webbing.

Pictured at right: Koi Fish Appliqued Jeans. A purchased iron-on koi fish applique makes a colorful embellishment for a jeans back pocket.

Iron-On Fabric Appliques

Available in many fabric departments as well as craft departments, you can find fusible fabric as well as pre-cut iron-on appliqué designs. Using iron-on (fusible) fabric is an easy, fast way to create all kinds of customized appliques. The fabric can be cut with scissors into almost any shape – you can use patterns, stencils, cookie cutters, or your own line drawings to create the shapes.

You can also make appliques from any fabric that can withstand the heat of ironing using fusible webbing. Simply cut the fabric and the fusible webbing to the same shape and iron-on.

Fabric glue can also be used to glue appliqués to jeans. Be sure to buy the type of glue that is made for fabric and is washable.

A simple car shape is created with two squares and two circles.

Four hearts of different sizes are arranged on a pocket. (You could cut out the same shapes in green and position them closer together to make a four-leaf clover.)

Four hearts create a diagonal line across a pocket.

Three flowers in three colors are placed in an overlapping arrangement.

Use a hot tool (found in craft or fabric departments) to apply iron-on appliqués. They are easy to use and save the mess of getting out the iron and ironing board.

Pictured at right: Twining Vines Jeans. A two-color purchased iron-on embroidered applique of vines and leaves enhances a turned-back cuff.

Daisies Galore Jeans

Embroidered iron-on appliques in two motifs – daisies and butterflies in a variety of sizes – are colorful, quick embellishments for these jeans. The jeans can be dry cleaned or hand washed, then air-dried. Appliques without iron-on backing can be glued in place with a washable, permanent fabric glue.

Designed by Patty Cox

SUPPLIES

Jeans

Iron-on embroidered appliqués:
  Daisies
  Butterflies

TOOLS

Iron

Pressing cloth

INSTRUCTIONS

1. Position iron-on appliques on jeans. Use the photo as a guide or try different arrangements until the result pleases you.
2. Using a press cloth, press each applique in position for 10 to 15 seconds to "tack" it in place. Let cool.
3. Turn jeans inside out. Press the back of each applique for 20 to 25 seconds to bond securely. ❏

Roses & Toile Jeans

Here, a black and white toile print fabric is paired with rose-motif embroidered appliques. You could customize the look – and change the colors – by choosing a different fabric or a different type of applique. After decorating, these jeans should be hand-washed and air-dried. These jeans use the "Cut and Wash" distressing technique shown on page 11.

Designed by Kirsten Jones

SUPPLIES

Jeans

2 rose-motif embroidered iron-on appliques

1/4 yd. toile fabric

Fabric glue

TOOLS

Scissors

Iron

INSTRUCTIONS

1. Cut holes in jeans, using the photo as a guide for placement. The holes you cut should be a little smaller than the desired final size.

2. Wash and dry the jeans two to three times to create frayed edges on the holes.

3. Cut a piece of fabric a little larger than each hole. Glue the fabric behind the holes on the inside of the jeans to create the peek-a-boo patches. Let the glue dry.

4. Apply the embroidered rose appliques as shown in photo, ironing them in place according to the package instructions. ❏

Doilies & Beads Jeans

Crocheted doilies create circles of color on jeans – you can use doilies of one color or choose two or more colors and mix them up like this pair. Doilies made from variegated thread have a tie-dyed look. If you're handy with a crochet needle, you can make them yourself, or you can buy plain white or ecru doilies and dye them to achieve the same effect.

The pointed edging on the outside of each doily is accented with gold seed beads. Stitching the beads anchors the doilies in place.

Designed by Patty Cox

SUPPLIES

Jeans

9 round crocheted doilies, 3-1/2" diameter (made of variegated thread or dyed)

Gold seed beads

Beading thread

Wash-away spray adhesive

TOOLS

Beading needle

Pictured above: The doilies.

INSTRUCTIONS

1. Arrange the doilies on the jeans using the photo as a guide.
2. Spray the backs of the doilies with wash-away spray adhesive. Re-position the doilies on the jeans.
3. Secure doilies in place by sewing a gold seed bead at each doily point with beading thread. ❏

Pictured at left: A doily is positioned part-way inside a back pocket.

Piccadilly Circus Jeans

Designed by Patty Cox

These jeans are reminiscent of the 1960s, when Piccadilly Circus in London was the stomping grounds for some of Britain's most famous pop stars. The Beatles' film *Help* had its world premiere at the London Pavilion at Piccadilly Circus, the city's entertainment hub, which is located at the junction of five busy streets. This retro print fantasy floral fabric recalls prints that were popular in the 60s.

SUPPLIES

Jeans

Denim scraps

2/3 yd. floral print fabric

Fusible web

10 buttons, 1/2" diameter

Embroidery floss, lavender

Washable permanent fabric glue (fabric bond)

Sewing thread

TOOLS

Iron

Sewing machine

Embroidery needle

Sewing needle

Seam ripper

INSTRUCTIONS

Fabric Insets on Legs:

1. Cut two pieces of fabric, each 12" x 18".

2. Fold under the bottom (12" edge) of one piece 1/4". Press. Fold under 1/4" again. Press and topstitch to hem. Repeat on other piece.

3. To make the pleats, crease or mark the fabric lengthwise in 2" increments. (Fig. 1) Press outer 2" folds to center. (Fig. 2) Set aside.

4. Open side seams of jeans legs, 15" long from the hem to end of opening. Make a diagonal cut on each side, measuring 1" down from point of opening. Make the cuts 1/2" deep. (Fig. 3)

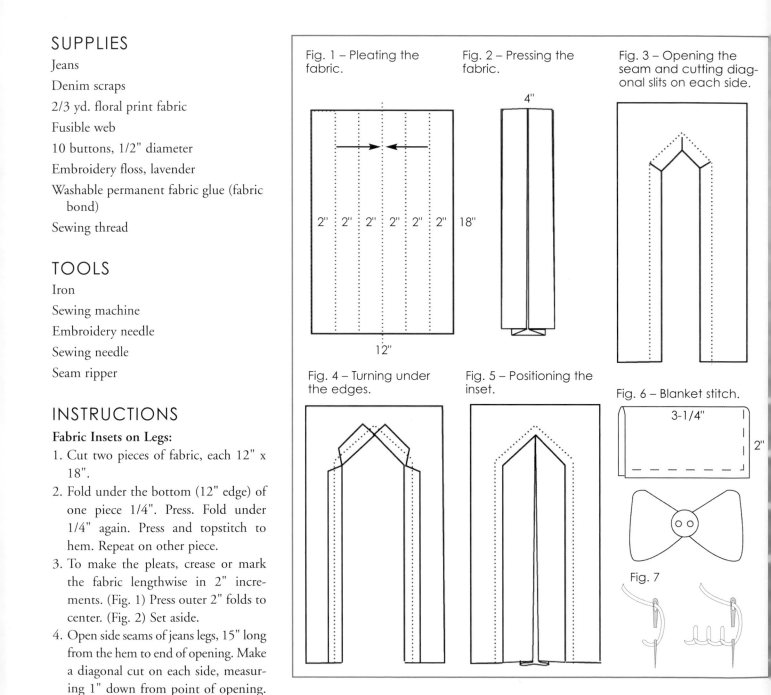

Fig. 1 – Pleating the fabric.

Fig. 2 – Pressing the fabric.

Fig. 3 – Opening the seam and cutting diagonal slits on each side.

Fig. 4 – Turning under the edges.

Fig. 5 – Positioning the inset.

Fig. 6 – Blanket stitch.

Fig. 7

5. Turn raw denim edges under and press. Topstitch. (Fig. 4) Repeat for other leg.

6. Apply fabric bond along top and side edges of pleated inset. Position inset inside jeans leg, aligning hems. Repeat for other side. Topstitch fabric in place. (Fig. 5)

Denim Bows:

1. Cut two pieces denim, each 3-1/4" x 4". Fold to make a piece 3-1/4" x 2". (Fig. 6) With right sides together, sew 1/4" seam along the long edge and one short edge. Turn right side out. Fold raw edge to inside 1/4". Whipstitch open end closed.

2. Make a running stitch across the center of each turned piece. Pull threads to gather tightly. Tie off threads.

3. Sew a button on bow center to secure gathers. (Fig. 6)

4. Sew a bow at the point where each pleated inset begins.

Appliques:

1. Apply fusible web on wrong side of remaining fabric. Cut out individual flower motifs to make appliques.

2. Remove the paper backing from the fusible web. Position appliques on jeans, using the photo as a guide, and iron in place.

3. Blanket stitch around each applique, using three strands embroidery floss. (Fig. 7)

4. Sew 1/2" buttons at the centers of some appliques. ❑

Lacy Flared Jeans

Green lace fabric is used to make insets, overlays, and appliques for these jeans. Placing the lace over skintone fabric gives the look of a cutout. Green seed beads are scattered over the front upper legs.

Designed by Patty Cox

SUPPLIES

Jeans

2/3 yd. green lace fabric, 45" wide

Skin-tone cotton fabric

Wash-away spray adhesive *or* glue stick

Washable permanent fabric glue (fabric bond)

Embroidery floss, green

Green seed beads

Green faceted beads, 3mm

Beading thread

TOOLS

Beading needle

Scissors

Seam ripper

Sewing machine

Measuring tape

Straight pins

INSTRUCTIONS

Lace Insets:

1. Open the side seam of each jeans leg 15" from the hem. Turn raw edges under 1/4". Machine topstitch the turned edges.

2. Cut two pieces of lace, each 10" x 16", making the bottom edge of each piece the finished edge of the lace. Gather each piece along the top (10") edge.

3. Place one lace section inside each jeans leg at the opened side seam with the gathered edge at the top and the finished edge even with the hem of the jeans. Pin in position.

Photo 1 – Lace placed over skin-tone fabric.

Photo 2 – Applique cutout.

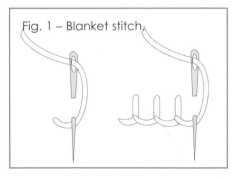

Fig. 1 – Blanket stitch.

4. Hand or machine stitch the lace inset to the open side seams. Repeat for other leg.

Lace Overlays:

1. Measure width of jeans lower leg 15" above the hem. Cut two pieces of lace as wide as the lower leg measurement + 1" (each piece will be approximately 15" x 15").

2. Following the floral pattern of the lace, shape the top edge of the lace piece, forming a V-shape. Repeat on other lace panel.

3. Using wash-away spray adhesive or a glue stick, adhere the lace panel around the lower part of each jeans leg, using the photo as a guide and aligning the lower edge of the lace with the hem of the jeans.

4. Hand stitch the edges of the lace panels to the jeans legs.

Lace Appliques:

1. Place lace on skin-tone cotton fabric. (Photo 1) Machine zig-zag around a six floral motifs to make appliques. Cut out. (Photo 2)

2. Position appliques on legs of jeans, above each gathered inset, using the photo as a guide. Secure in place with fabric glue.

3. When the glue has dried, blanket stitch around each applique using three strands embroidery floss. (Fig. 1)

Beads:

Sew seed beads and faceted beads in a scattered pattern on jeans top. Knot thread on inside of jeans beneath each bead. ❑

Patchwork Fantasy Jacket

Color is the unifying theme for this jacket. You can make your own patchwork fabric or salvage part of an old quilt top for the yoke decoration. Doilies were colored with fabric dye to match the patchwork. Fabric yo-yos and ribbon roses are additional decorative elements. Gold sequin trim and gold buttons are bright metallic accents.

Designed by Patty Cox

SUPPLIES

Jeans jacket

Burgundy patchwork fabric

Assorted small crocheted doilies

Ribbon roses

1/4 yd. red or burgundy fabric

Gold sequin spooled trim

Seed beads

Beading thread

6 bright gold buttons, 3/8"

Tracing paper

Washable permanent fabric glue (fabric bond)

Jewelry glue

TOOLS

Pencil

Scissors

Beading needle

Hand sewing needle

Craft knife

Iron

Optional: Sewing machine

INSTRUCTIONS

Yoke:

1. Lay tracing paper over the front yoke of the jacket. Trace yoke shape on tracing paper to make a pattern. Cut out the pattern. (Photo 1)
2. Place pattern on patchwork fabric. Cut fabric 3/4" larger than pattern on all sides. (Photo 2) Reverse (flip) pattern and cut a second yoke applique from patchwork fabric for the other side.
3. Turn under raw edges of yoke fabric 3/4". Press. Pin in place and check fit.
4. Hand sew applique fabric to yoke, allowing the fabric to cover button or snaps.

If your jacket has buttons, use a craft knife to cut a horizontal slit over each button and bring the button through the slit, then whipstitch the slit closed under button around the shank. On the opposite yoke (the one with the buttonholes), hand or machine stitch new buttonholes over the existing buttonholes, using matching thread. Slit the centers of the new buttonholes with a craft knife.

If your jacket has snap closures, allow the fabric to cover the snaps on the side with the tops of the snaps. On the other side, carefully trim away the fabric around the snap, then use fabric glue to adhere the cut edges of the fabric around the snaps.

Cuff Trim:

1. Trace the cuff trim pattern provided and cut out. Cut one cuff trim piece from patchwork fabric, then reverse the pattern and cut another cuff trim piece from the patchwork fabric.
2. Turn under the cuff trim raw fabric edges 3/4". Press.
3. Pin the cuff trim pieces on the sleeves, aligning the turned edges with the cuffs and the sleeve openings.
4. Hand sew cuff trim fabric pieces in place.

Continued on page 40

Photo 1 – The front yoke of the jacket with the tracing paper pattern in place, *left,* and the fabric applique cut from the pattern placed on the jacket, *right.*

Photo 2 – The pattern on the applique fabric. The fabric is 3/4" larger on all sides than the pattern.

PATCHWORK JACKET

continued from page 38

Sequins:

1. Transfer sequin swirl patterns to jacket front. Apply jewelry glue on transferred lines. Place a string of sequins on the glue.

2. Transfer the smaller swirl pattern to the sleeves above the cuff trim. Glue lines of sequins to the sleeves.

3. Glue a line of sequin trim around the collar edge. Allow to dry.

Yo-Yos:

1. Cut four 2" fabric circles and four 3" fabric circles. Turn outer raw edge under 1/8". Press.

2. Working one circle at a time, hand sew running stitches around the turned edge of each one. Pull the gathering stitches tightly and knot the thread to secure. Flatten slightly with the gathers in the center.

Applying Embellishments

1. *Optional:* Dye doilies to match fabric. Let dry.

2. Arrange doilies, ribbon roses, and yo-yos on jacket front, using the photo as a guide.

3. Apply fabric glue on backs of yo-yos and doilies. Press into position on jacket. Allow to dry.

4. Using a beading needle and beading thread, sew a seed bead at the beginning and end of each row of sequins.

5. Sew a seed bead at each point on the edges of the doilies.

6. Sew gold buttons in the center of each yo-yo. ❑

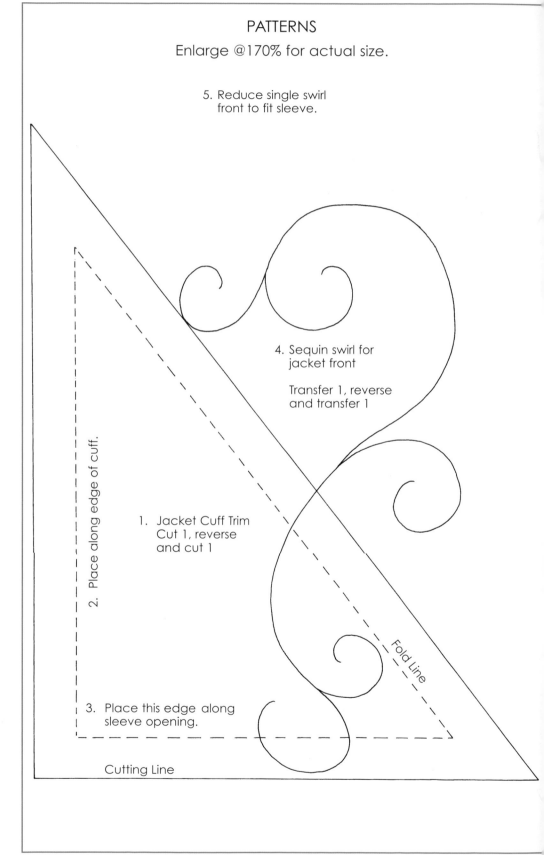

PATTERNS

Enlarge @170% for actual size.

5. Reduce single swirl front to fit sleeve.

4. Sequin swirl for jacket front

Transfer 1, reverse and transfer 1

2. Place along edge of cuff.

1. Jacket Cuff Trim Cut 1, reverse and cut 1

Fold Line

3. Place this edge along sleeve opening.

Cutting Line

ART DECO INSPIRATION JACKET

Instructions begin on page 42.

Patterns
Actual Size

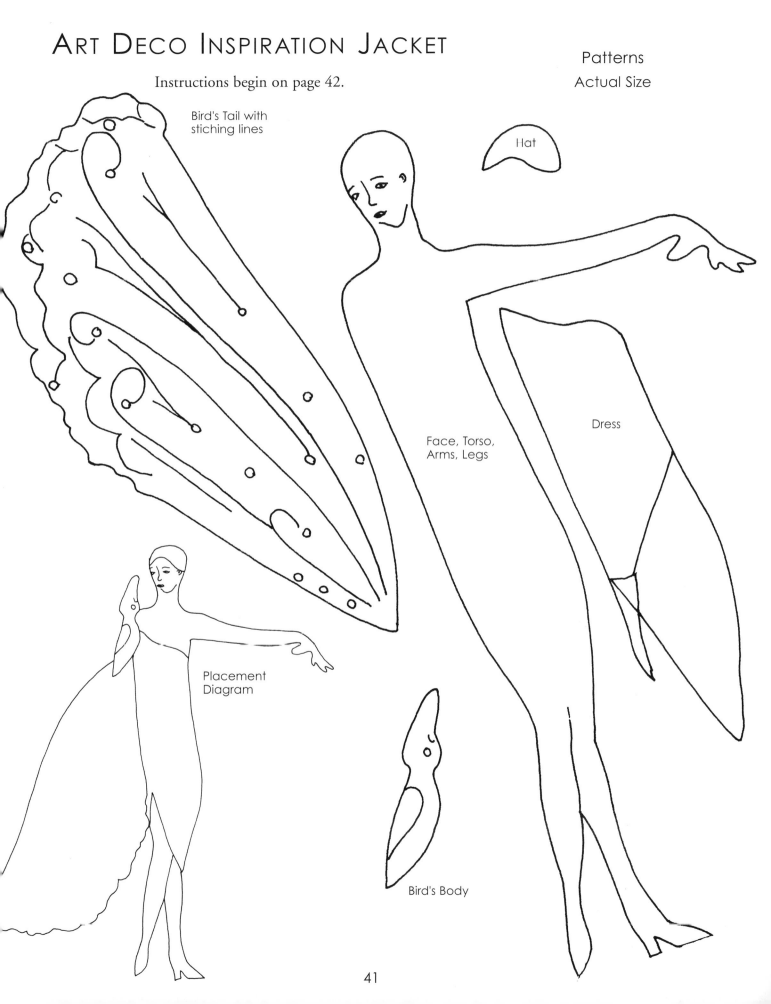

Bird's Tail with
stiching lines

Hat

Face, Torso,
Arms, Legs

Dress

Placement
Diagram

Bird's Body

Art Deco Inspiration Jacket

An Erte lithograph from the 1920s was the inspiration for this jacket applique, created with cutouts of fusible synthetic suede and decorated with machine embroidery and fusible crystals. Fine-tip markers were used to add details to the appliques.

Designed by Abby Riba

Patterns appear on page 41.

SUPPLIES

Jeans jacket

Fusible synthetic suede:

Bright blue

White

Beige

Black

Fine-tip permanent markers:

Brown

Green

Purple

Red

Fusible crystals, 3mm size:

Clear

Gold

Black

Thread for machine embroidery – Red, gold

Tracing paper

Transfer paper

TOOLS

Straight pins

Pencil

Sewing machine with decorative stitch capability

Hot-fix applicator tool (for crystals)

Stylus

INSTRUCTIONS

1. Trace the patterns onto tracing paper and cut out. Pin paper patterns to the various colors of fusible suede fabric:
   • Face, torso, arms; legs – Beige
   • Dress – Black
   • Hat – White
   • Bird's tail – Bright blue
   • Bird's body – White
2. Transfer to the fabric using transfer paper the following lines:
   • Outline and the stitching lines for the bird's tail feathers
   • Outline and separation line on dress.
   • Outline of hat.
   Do not cut out fabric pieces yet.
3. Remove paper pattern from dress and hat. Using red thread, decorate the skirt potion of the dress with rows of straight stitching. Stitch the dress bodice and hat with rows of honeycomb stitching. Add a row of satin stitching at the waistline of the dress to cover the beginnings of the rows of stitches.
4. Remove the paper pattern from bird's tail. Using gold thread, add decorative stitches to bird's tail with straight and satin stitches.
5. Cut out the fabric pattern pieces from the various fusible suede colors.
6. Position the beige skintone pieces on the back of the jacket. Press to fuse.
7. Position the remaining pieces and press in place. Let cool.
8. Use the permanent markers to add shoes, facial features, details on legs and hand, and bird.
9. Decorate with fusible crystals, using the photo as a guide for placement. ❏

Stones, Studs & Beads

Stones, studs, and beads add three-dimensional texture, metallic shine, and sparkle to jeans. The application process varies according to the type of embellishment you're using.

Hot-fix adhesive-backed rhinestones that are attached with a hot-fix applicator or an iron are so much fun and easy to apply to your jeans. You can also attach flat-backed, non-adhesive rhinestones, studs, and jewels with a mechanical setting tool. Other accents, such as beads, can be attached with beading thread. Another option is to glue jewels and embellishments to jeans using a permanent jewel glue.

Pictured at right: Rhinestone Branch Jeans. A green iron-on rhinestone branch adds sparkle and color to the back pocket of a pair of jeans.

Attaching Self-Adhesive Stones

Using a hot-fix applicator tool to attach flat-backed hot-fix rhinestones is quick and easy. There are several models available – they work much like a simple soldering iron. Most of the applicators come with different tips to accommodate the various sizes of stones. If the tip isn't the correct size for a stone you are using, the stone can be placed with tweezers. If you are using nailheads and studs you will need to place them with tweezers.

1. Use the appropriate size tip on your applicator tool for the rhinestone size. Plug in your applicator tool. Place your rhinestones, face up on a hard flat surface. Pick up a stone with the applicator tool.

2. Wait a few seconds. The heat sensitive glue o the back of the stones will begin to melt and shine. Smaller stones take less time to melt.

3. As soon as the glue starts to look shiny, place the applicator straight down on the fabric surface. Allow the stone to touch the fabric, but the applicator tip should not touch the surface. The stone will be released from the applicator and attach to the fabric. Lift the applicator tool immediately.

4. *Option:* You can also place stones, studs, and nailheads with tweezers.

5. Heat the embellishments with the tool to set. Some tools have a flat tip for metal embellishments or jewel cut rhinestones.

Iron-On Studs

Use iron-on studs to create lines and patterns of circles, squares, dashes, and teardrop shapes. One easy, simple way to use them is to embellish a pocket. Here are five examples applied to pocket-shaped denim pieces.

A row of alternating circles and squares.

A row of circles with pearly centers.

A row of circles with open centers.

A row of rectangles looks like a dotted line.

A swirl of closely spaced circles.

Setting Stones & Studs with a Setting Tool

There are a wide variety of setting tools for rhinestones and studs. Earlier hand tools were sized for each individual type and size of stone and setting. Newer versions are typically sold with adapters so they can be used with a wide range of stone and setting sizes and a variety of shapes.

Plunger-type setters are easy to use – you place the setting, place the stone, put the setter in place, and press. Staple-type (their name comes from their resemblance to desktop staplers) work in much the same way.

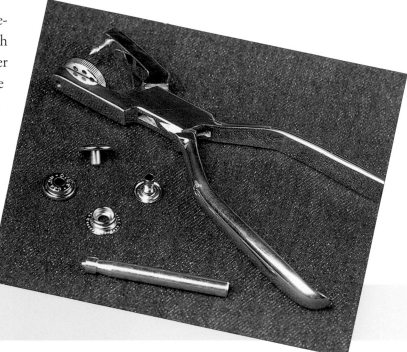

SETTING SNAPS

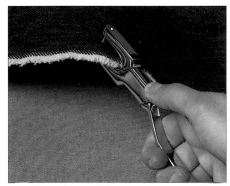

1. Punch a hole into fabric with a hole punch.

2. Place the front part of the snap.

Pictured above: This photo shows a hole punch and a setting tool for snaps and studs.

3. Place the back part of the snap.

4. Set snap using setting tool

First part of snap is in place. Repeat procedure for setting the matching section of snap.

49

SETTING STONES

Basic Instructions

1. Place the rhinestone prong setting on the setter pin with the prongs pointed down toward the cup of the setter.
2. Place a rhinestone into the cup of the setter with the rhinestone face (faceted side) down.
3. Position fabric right side down over cup.
4. Firmly press down on the setter handle so the prongs enter the fabric evenly and clinch rhinestone in place.

Option: To view the arrangement of the stones on the front of the jeans before setting, glue the stones in place with jewelry glue.. Allow glue to dry. Put the setting in the setter and position the stone – with fabric attached – in the cup of the setter. Press down to set.

The stone setting tool.

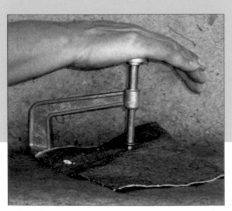

The rhinestone setter is worked on the back of the fabric.

ON THE BORDERS JEANS

Rows of iron-on studs, available in a variety of colors and shapes, are a great way to emphasize the edges of pockets and flaps. Studs can be applied with an iron or with a hot-fix tool. Use more than one color for a custom look.

Gluing Stones & Beads

SPARKLING FLOWERS JEANS

A flower of iron-on studs and rhinestones add sparkle and shine to a jeans leg. You can group the motifs or scatter them randomly.

Jewelry glue can be used to attach stones and studs. Simply hold embellishment with a pair of tweezers, place a dot of glue on the back of the stone or place a dot of glue on the fabric. Then place the stone. It's as easy as that.

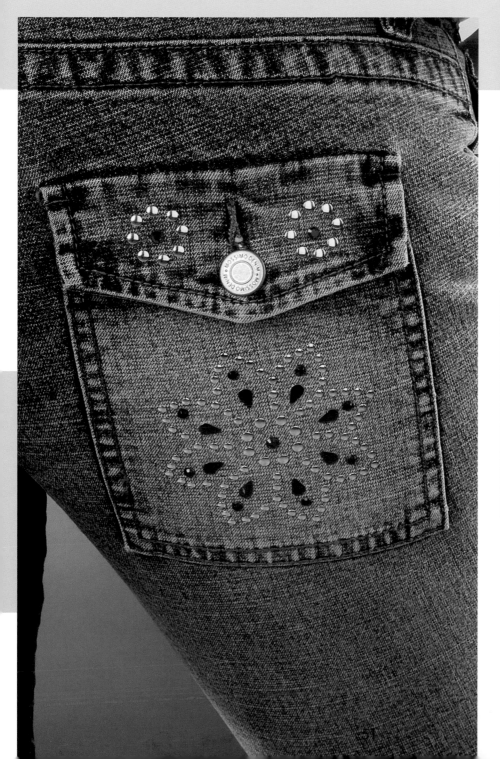

Placing a dot of glue on the fabric.

Stone with glue on the back is placed.

Brass Stud Swirls

Brass spots – another name for studs – are available in multiple sizes and shapes and come in packages of various sizes, from a few dozen pieces to a thousand. Use the spot manufacturer's recommended setting tools for best results. Here, brass spots of various sizes are placed in swirls and accented with frosted cabochons, which are glued in place.

Designed by Patty Cox

Pattern
Actual Size

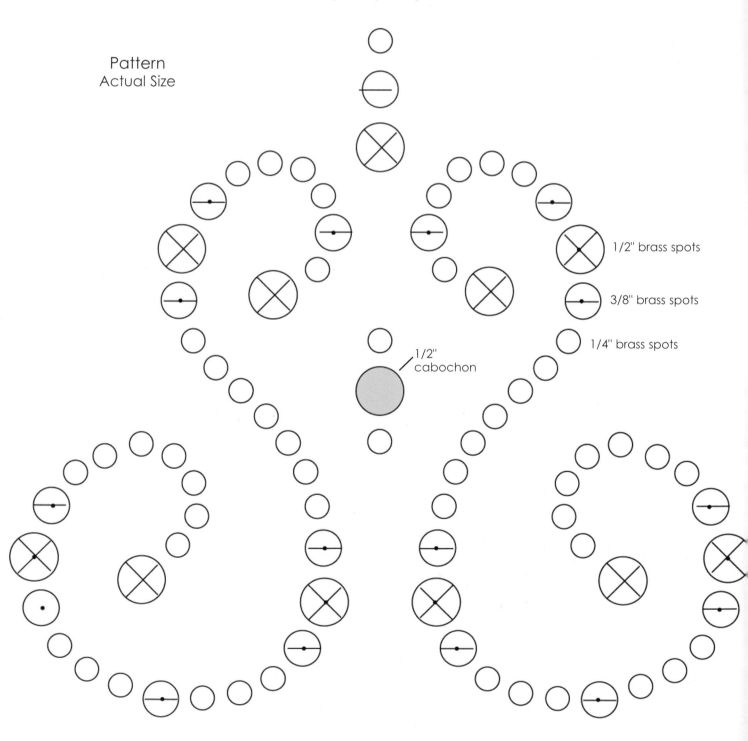

1/2" brass spots

3/8" brass spots

1/4" brass spots

1/2" cabochon

SUPPLIES

Jeans

Brass spots:

   76 – 1/2"

   118 – 3/8"

   368 – 1/4"

6 gold frosted cabochons, 1/2"

Bridal tulle

Black permanent marker

White chalk *or* white dressmaker's
   pencil

Jewelry glue

Tracing paper

TOOLS

Needlenose pliers *or* spot setter

INSTRUCTIONS

1. Trace pattern. Enlarge on a photocopier.
2. Transfer pattern to outside of jeans legs. See "Transferring Patterns" for instructions.
3. Attach the brass spots to the jeans using needlenose pliers or a spot setter to attach them to the setting.
4. Glue the cabochons between swirls along the side seams.

Rhinestone & Ribbon Jeans

A wide pink brocade ribbon was used to trim the turned-up cuffs of these jeans.
Pink and crystal clear rhinestones in a variety of sizes decorate the tops of the legs.
See the beginning of this section for information about setting rhinestones.

Designed by Patty Cox

SUPPLIES

Jeans

Rhinestones and studs in a variety of sizes – 8mm, 6mm, 4-1/2mm, in pink and crystal

1/2 yd. pink brocade ribbon, 18" wide

Pink sewing thread

Jewelry glue

TOOLS

Rhinestone setter

Sewing needle

INSTRUCTIONS

Rhinestones:

Follow this process to set each rhinestone.

1. Place rhinestone prong setting on setter pin with the prongs pointed down toward the cup of the setter.
2. Place a rhinestone, face down, into the cup of the setter.
3. Position fabric, right side down, over the cup. Firmly press down setter handle so prongs enter the fabric evenly and clinch rhinestone in place.

Optional Method: To arrange the stones on the front of the jeans before setting, glue stones on jeans with jewelry glue. Allow glue to dry. Follow the instructions above to set the rhinestones, placing the stone (with the fabric attached) in the setter cup.

Ribbon:

1. Turn up bottoms of legs about 3" to form cuffs.
2. Stitch ribbon over the outer leg seam, turning raw edges under. ❏

Random Rhinestone Jeans

Using a permanent jewelry glue is a quick, easy way to decorate jeans with rhinestones and other flat-backed gems. After the glue is dry, the jeans can be hand washed and line dried, but not dry cleaned.

Designed by Patty Cox

SUPPLIES

Jeans

Flat-back rhinestones and gems in various sizes – 8mm, 6mm, 4-1/2mm, in blue, green, and turquoise

Jewel glue

INSTRUCTIONS

Arrange rhinestones on fronts of legs and along side seams at the bottoms of legs and glue in place. Allow glue to dry. ❏

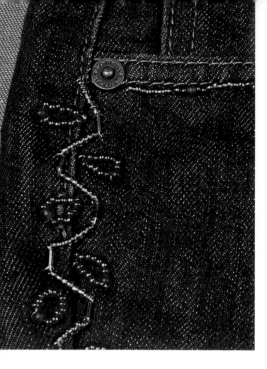

Beaded Vines Jeans

Sewing beads is simple – just be sure to use a beading needle (one with an eye small enough to fit through the holes in the beads without straining) and beading thread, which is stronger and more durable than regular sewing thread.

Adding fringe to the bottom is a good way to add length to jeans that are too short. The three layers used here create a lush look.

Designed by Patty Cox

SUPPLIES

Jeans

Seed beads, reddish pink, green

1/4" bugle beads, green

E-beads, red

Beading thread

3-1/2 yds. washable suede fringe, 3" wide

Sewing thread (to match fringe)

TOOLS

Beading needle

Sewing machine

INSTRUCTIONS

Fringe:

Determine how long you want the jeans to be, and position the fringe accordingly.

1. Place the top of the suede fringe along the bottom of one leg of the jeans. Machine sew the top edge of the fringe to the jeans, overlapping the ends 1/4" at the inner seam. Cut the end.
2. Stitch a second row of fringe just above the first. Overlap the end 1/4" and cut.
3. Add a third layer just above the second to make three overlapping layers in all.
4. Repeat for other leg.

Beaded Vines:

The vines are made of green beads. See Fig. 2.

1. Thread needle with beading thread and knot one end. Bring up needle from inside of one jeans leg on the outside seam above the fringe. Add seven green seed beads on needle. Thread needle back through jeans so the seed beads are in a diagonal line.
2. Bring needle back up. Add a green bugle bead. Thread needle back through jeans. Knot thread inside jeans.
3. Bring up needle. Add seven green seed beads. Thread needle back through jeans so the seed beads are on a diagonal line in the opposite direction.
4. Continue adding beads to the zig-zag stem, using the side seam of the jeans as a guide.
5. To made the beaded design more durable, run beading thread back through the beads. Knot thread inside jeans.
6. Repeat on other leg.

Beaded Flowers:

The flowers are loops of reddish pink and red beads.

1. Thread needle with beading thread and knot one end. Bring up needle from inside jeans hem near the top of the first bugle bead. Add seven reddish pink seed beads, one red e-bead, and six reddish pink seed beads. (Fig. 1) Thread needle back through the first bead and through the jeans, creating a loop of beads.
2. Position loop at an angle as shown in Fig. 2. Bring up the needle through the e-bead, then back down through jeans. Knot thread inside jeans, but do not cut the thread.
3. Continue adding beaded flowers next to each green bugle bead on the vine.
4. Repeat on the other leg.

Beaded Pocket Trim:

1. Thread the needle with beading thread and knot one end. Bring up the needle from inside the edge of the front pocket. Add seven green seed beads.
2. Thread needle down through pocket edge, then back up. Add two reddish pink seed beads, a red e-bead, and two reddish pink seed beads. Thread needle down through pocket edge. Knot thread.
3. Bring up needle and continue adding beads in the same sequence along the pocket edge. Knot the thread on the inside of the pocket when you reach the end. Cut thread.
4. Repeat on other front pocket. ❑

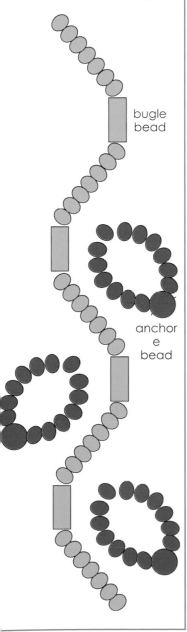

Fig. 1 – Stringing the beads to make the bead loop.

6 beads

e bead

6 beads

Fig. 2 – The vine and flower bead pattern for the legs.

bugle bead

anchor e bead

Crystal Bouquet Jeans

A flower bouquet of sparkling crystals decorates the lower part of one leg of these jeans. These jeans were inspired by jeans the designer saw in a store window in Paris. The jeans legs were encrusted with crystals in various designs – with a price tag of $1000 US. Making your own is much more creative and less expensive – and you can customize. This design uses hot-fix rhinestones attached with a hot fix applicator tool.

Designed by Abby Riba

SUPPLIES

Jeans

4mm flat-backed hot-fix rhinestones, blue, pink, green

3mm flat-backed hot-fix rhinestones, light blue, pale pink, light green

White transfer paper

Tracing paper

TOOLS

Pencil

Stylus

Hot-fix applicator

INSTRUCTIONS

1. Trace the pattern. Transfer to the lower part of one jeans leg.
2. Insert the tip for 4mm stones and heat the applicator. Using the photo as a guide, set the flower outlines with blue and pink hot-fix rhinestones and the leaf stems and veins with green.
3. Switch to the tip for 3mm stones and fill in the flowers with light blue and pale pink hot-fix rhinestones. Outline and fill in the leaf shapes with light green hot-fix rhinestones. ❏

Pattern
Enlarge @175% for actual size.

Embroidery

Embroidery uses thread or yarn to create designs and motifs, which can be outlined or filled in solidly with stitchery. Whether done by hand or machine, embroidery is a way to add color, texture, and decoration to jeans.

Leather-Lettered Jeans

Wear your initial on your leg! A leather monogram is enhanced with an embroidered scroll design and copper seed beads. Make the pattern for your initial by tracing a letter from a clip art book or printing one on your computer.

Designed by Patty Cox

Pictured on page 61.

SUPPLIES

Jeans

Thin leather, 5" square

Fusible web

Embroidery floss, dark gold

Seed beads, copper

Black beading thread

Letter pattern (see above.)

Tracing paper

Bridal tulle

Dressmaker's chalk

Sewing thread to match leather

TOOLS

Embroidery hoop

Embroidery needle

Beading needle

Pencil

Iron

Scissors *or* craft knife

Sewing machine

Optional: Seam ripper

INSTRUCTIONS

1. Trace the scroll pattern. Position the letter on the scroll pattern to find an attractive arrangement. Reverse or turn the scroll pattern as needed to best accent the letter. Transfer scroll pattern to the jeans. See "Transferring Patterns."

Pattern
Actual Size

2. Reverse the monogram letter and transfer to the paper side of fusible web. Iron fusible web on the back of the leather square.

3. Cut out monogram letter. Remove paper backing. Position letter over scroll pattern on jeans. *Option:* Open about 12" of the side seam of the jeans to simplify machine sewing in step 5.

4. Iron letter in place.

5. Machine zig-zag letter with matching thread to attach it to jeans.

6. Thread embroidery needle with three strands of embroidery floss. Stem stitch the scroll pattern.

7. Thread beading needle with black beading thread. Sew copper seed beads around the embroidered design according to the pattern.

8. If you opened the jeans seam, re-sew it. ❏

Free-Form Rose Appliques

You can make custom embroidered appliques in the motifs and colors of your choice. You need a zig-zag sewing machine, a pattern, and an embroidery hoop to hold the fabric taut as you work. You can glue or sew the appliques in place, or use fusible web to iron them on your jeans.
Using fabric stabilizer under the printed fabric makes it easier to move the fabric while you're embroidering.

Designed by Patty Cox

SUPPLIES

Lightweight cotton fabric

3 colors of thread in a range of pink and red tones

Lightweight fabric stabilizer sheet

Washable permanent fabric glue (fabric bond)

Tracing paper

Transfer paper

TOOLS

Sewing machine

Embroidery hoop

Pencil

Stylus

Scissors

INSTRUCTIONS

1. Cut a square of fabric to fit your embroidery hoop. Cut a piece of stabilizer the same size as the fabric.

2. Trace the pattern and transfer the design to the fabric.

3. Place the fabric square with the transferred design on top of the stabilizer. Secure in the embroidery hoop, centering the design in the embroidery hoop so the fabric and stabilizer will lie flat against the surface of the sewing machine.

4. Remove the presser foot from your sewing machine. Slide the embroidery hoop with the fabric under the needle. Place flat on the sewing machine surface, under the presser foot post. Lower the presser foot post.

5. Thread the machine with the darkest color thread. Set the machine to a narrow zig-zag stitch. Machine zig-zag over the pattern outlines, using both hands to guide the embroidery hoop under the needle. Turn the hoop as you stitch satin stitches that point toward the outside of the hoop. (Photo 1) Raise presser foot post. Trim threads.

Photo 1 – The outlines stitched with the darkest color thread.

Continued on page 64

FREE-FORM ROSE APPLIQUES

continued from page 63

Pattern
Enlarge @140%
for actual size.

6. Thread the machine with the lightest color thread. Lower presser foot post. Machine zig-zag stitch the highlights, butting the zig-zag highlight stitches against the outline stitches. (Photo 2) Raise presser foot post. Trim threads.

7. Thread the machine with the medium color thread. Lower presser foot post. Machine zig-zag the midtone areas, overlapping the stitches to fill in all midtone areas. (Photo 3) Raise presser foot post. Trim threads.

8. Thread machine with the darkest color thread again. Lower the presser foot post. Go over the rose outline a second time to reinforce the design. (Photo 4) Raise presser foot post. Trim threads. Slide embroidery hoop from under presser foot.

9. Remove the fabric from the embroidery hoop. Cut out the applique close to the edge of the design.

10. Machine zig-zag around the outer edge of the design with the darkest color thread. (Photo 5) Trim the thread.

To apply: Spread fabric glue on the applique back. Position the applique on the denim surface. Finger press in place. *Option:* Secure the outer edge by stitching by hand or machine, using a zig-zag stitch. ❑

Photo 2 – The highlights stitched with the lightest color thread.

Photo 3 – Midtone areas filled in with medium color thread.

Photo 4 – The outlines stitched a second time with the darkest color thread.

Photo 5 – The completed applique.

Rose Bouquet
Embroidered Fabric Appliques

Instead of using a line drawing as a pattern, you can embroider over a printed motif on a piece of fabric to create appliques for your jeans. Choose a fabric that includes motifs that are the size you want your appliques to be. Here a floral print that includes stylized roses and leaves was used as the base fabric. With this technique, you can choose to outline the motif only (leaving some of the printed design showing), or you can completely cover the motif with embroidery.

Designed by Patty Cox

SUPPLIES
Cotton print fabric

Wash-away fabric stabilizer sheet

Sewing thread in several colors, one for each color in the motif

Washable permanent fabric glue (fabric bond)

TOOLS
Sewing machine

Embroidery hoop

Scissors

INSTRUCTIONS
1. Cut a square of the base fabric (Photo 1) to fit your embroidery hoop. Cut a piece of stabilizer the same size.

2. Place the fabric square on top of the wash-away stabilizer in the embroidery hoop, centering the design in the embroidery hoop with fabric and stabilizer flat against the surface.

3. Remove the presser foot from the sewing machine. Slide the embroidery hoop under the presser foot post with the stabilizer flat against the sewing machine surface. Lower presser foot post.

4. Thread the machine with the darkest color thread. Set the machine on zig-zag stitch and machine zig-zag over pattern outline. Use both hands to glide the hoop under the needle. Turn hoop while stitching, making stitches overlap and change direction. Raise the presser foot post. Trim thread. At this point, you can remove the applique from the embroidery hoop, trim it, and zig-zag stitch over the edge to complete the applique (Photo 2), or you can keep the fabric in the hoop and continue.

5. To make a solid thread applique like the one in Photo 3, thread the machine with the lightest color thread. Lower the presser foot post. Machine zig-zag the light areas of the motif, placing these zig-zag stitches against the outline stitches. Continue to fill in the design, changing threads to match the various areas until the fabric motif is completely covered. When you are finished, lift the presser foot post, remove the embroidery hoop, and trim the threads.

6. Cut out the applique close to the edge of the motif. Carefully cut away excess stabilizer. Machine zig-zag around the outer edge of the design. To remove the remaining stabilizer, follow the manufacturer's instructions.

To apply: Spread fabric glue on the back of the applique. Position the applique on the denim surface. Finger press in place. *Option:* Secure outer edge of design by stitching by hand or machine, using a zig-zag stitch. ❑

Using a fabric stabilizer under the printed fabric makes it easier to move the fabric while you're embroidering.

Photo 1 – The fabric chosen as the base for the applique.

Photo 2 – An applique made by outlining the fabric motif.

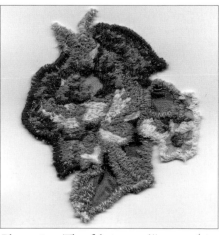
Photo 3 – The fabric motif covered in thread of several colors to make an applique.

Various floral motif appliques are grouped together on a pair of jeans.

Western Flair Jeans

This sophisticated one-color design is reminiscent of motifs on rodeo costumes and "ranch wear" popular in the 1940s and 50s. The split stitch is easy to work and the size of the yarn gives impact to the embroidered design.

Designed by Patty Cox

See page 68 for pattern.

SUPPLIES

Jeans

Light brown nylon yarn (This came in a 99-yd. skein.)

Bridal tulle

TOOLS

Sharp large-eye needle

Black fine-tip permanent marker

White chalk *or* white pencil

Liquid fray preventative

INSTRUCTIONS

1. Trace pattern. Enlarge to fit the fronts of your jeans legs.
2. Place bridal tulle over pattern. Trace pattern onto tulle with a marker. (Photo 1)
3. Position tulle on front of jeans leg. Trace over pattern with white chalk. (Photo 2)
4. Thread needle with nylon yarn. Knot thread end. Dot fray preventative on the short end of the yarn to keep it from raveling while you stitch. Insert needle from inside of jeans.
5. Embroider the design with a split stitch (Fig. 1), making stitches 1/4" to 3/8" long. Finish one area of the design, then knot yarn inside jeans. Dot knot with fray preventative.
6. Continue embroidering until both lower leg designs are complete.
7. Use chalk to draw a squiggly line along the edges of the curved front pockets.
8. Embroidered along the chalk lines, again using a split stitch. (Fig. 1) ❑

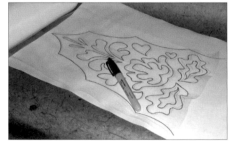

Photo 1 – Tracing the enlarged pattern onto bridal tulle.

Photo 2 – Using white chalk to transfer the design to a jeans leg.

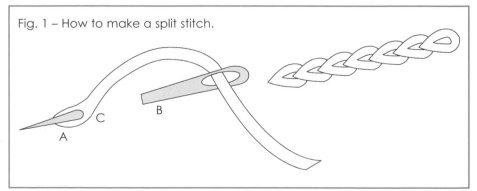

Fig. 1 – How to make a split stitch.

Pattern for Western Flair Jeans
Enlarge @ 120% for actual size

Shisha Sequin Embroidery Jeans

This embellishing idea borrows from a technique often used on Indian textiles –
decorating fabric with tiny mirrors bordered with hand-embroidered frames.
("Shisha" means mirror.) These jeans borrow the look, but the technique
is done differently: machine stitching is used for the frames, and large
sequins are used instead of mirrors.

Designed by Patty Cox

See page 72 for pattern.

SUPPLIES

Jeans

Black lightweight, tear-away stabilizer

Rayon thread, fuchsia, bright green

Silver sequins, 5mm and 10mm

Fuchsia seed beads

Washable permanent fabric glue (fabric bond)

Liquid fray preventative

Tracing paper

Bridal tulle

TOOLS

Pencil

Sewing machine

White dressmaker's pencil

White chalk

INSTRUCTIONS

1. Trace patterns and enlarge as needed to fit your jeans.
2. Transfer patterns to outer jeans legs and front pockets.
3. Set sewing machine stitch length to the highest number of stitches per inch and thread with green thread. Zig-zag green swirls, using rayon thread. Make a second layer of stitches over the first, building up layers of thread. Clip threads. Dot thread ends with fray preventative.
4. To make the sequin frames, use a white dressmaker's pencil to trace around a sequin on a piece of tear-away stabilizer. (Photo 1) Trace 18 circles in all.
5. Thread sewing machine with fuchsia rayon thread. Set sewing machine to the highest number of stitches per inch. Zig-zag around each circle. Make a second round of stitches over the first, building up layers of thread. Cut threads. Dot thread ends with fray preventative.
6. Tear stitched circles from stabilizer. Tear out centers. (Photo 2)
7. Glue zig-zagged circle frames on jeans according to pattern. Allow glue to dry. (Photo 2)
8. Using the fuchsia thread, zig-zag circles to jeans, using fewer stitches per inch.
9. Sew 10mm sequins inside the zig-zagged circle frames, using a seed bead to secure each sequin.
10. As shown on the pattern, sew 10mm and 5mm sequins with seed beads on jeans to complete the designs on the legs and the pocket edges. ❑

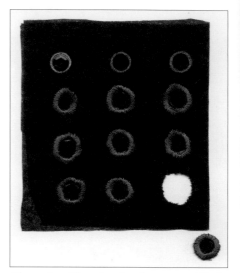

Photo 1 – The circular frames on fabric stabilizer – traced circles on the top row, embroidered on the bottom three rows, a circle torn away at bottom right.

Photo 2 – The circular frames applied to the jeans leg.

Shisha Sequin Embroidery Jeans

Patterns
Enlarge @200% for actual size.

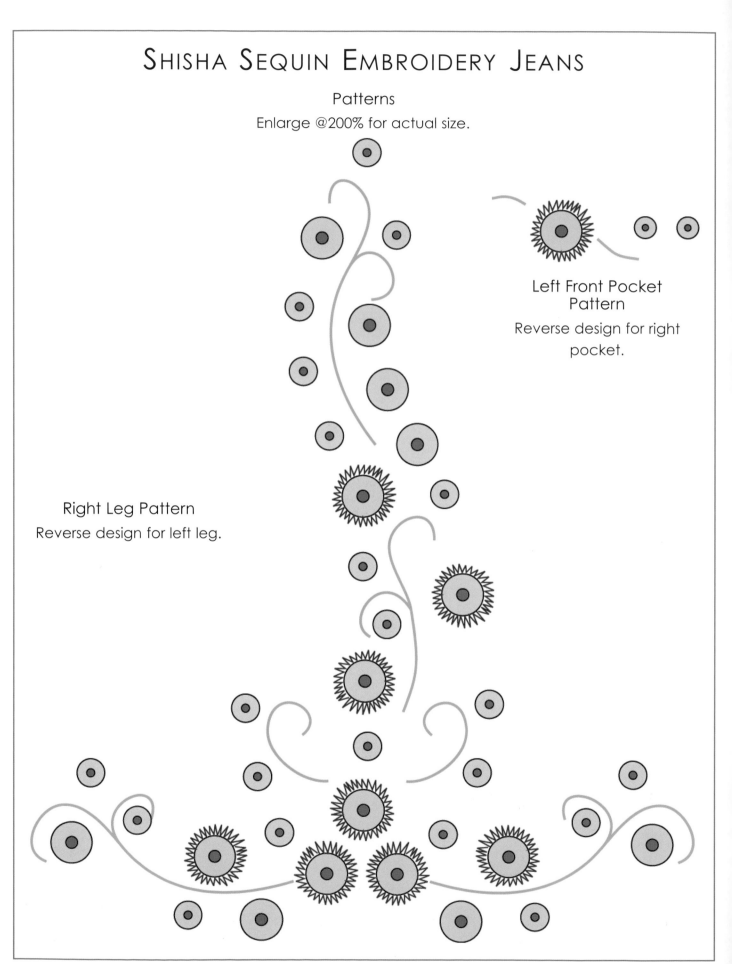

Left Front Pocket Pattern

Reverse design for right pocket.

Right Leg Pattern

Reverse design for left leg.

Bright Butterflies Jeans

Six brightly colored butterflies flutter on the leg of a pair of white jeans. The butterflies were machine-embroidered, using patterns from an embroidery disk, on different colors of fusible synthetic suede.

Designed by Abby Riba

Here's the process for each butterfly: Secure a piece of medium-to-heavy wash-away stabilizer sheet in an embroidery hoop, baste a piece of synthetic suede to the stabilizer, and machine embroider. Rinse away the stabilizer, using a toothbrush to scrub away the stabilizer inside the embroidery, and allow the synthetic suede to dry completely. Trim around the embroidered piece, leaving a border of 1/8" to 1/4" outside the embroidered outline to ensure secure fusing.

The stems and leaves were cut with a die cutter and fused to the jeans, following the suede manufacturer's instructions. The butterflies were arranged around the plant and fused in place.

73

Painting

Painted designs offer endless opportunity and variety for decorating jeans. A variety of paints specially formulated for painting on fabric are available at crafts and fabrics stores. They come in an array of colors, including metallics, and are water-washable when dry. Most call for heat-setting with an iron for added durability. Be sure to follow the manufacturer's instructions for best results.

You can also mix textile medium with acrylic craft paints to create permanent, washable painted effects on fabric.

Painted Daisies Jeans Jacket

Bright paint colors create a field of flowers on the yokes of this jacket. Two iron-on daisy appliques on the lower left front of the jacket are detailed with painted stems and small painted flowers. The jacket can be hand-washed.

Designed by Kirsten Jones

Pictured on page 75.

SUPPLIES

Jeans jacket

2 iron-on embroidered appliqués, daisies

Brush-on fabric paints:
    White
    Fresh foliage
    Coastal blue
    Lavender
    Vintage orange
    Sugar plum

Tracing paper

Transfer paper

TOOLS

#3 round paint brush
Iron
Stylus
Pencil

INSTRUCTIONS

1. Trace the pattern. Enlarge as needed. Transfer the design to the yokes of the jacket.
2. Paint the design (flowers, leaves, and stems), using the photo as a guide for color placement. Let dry.
3. Attach embroidered appliques at bottom front of jacket as shown, following the package instructions.
4. Paint stems and small flowers around the appliques. Let dry. ❏

Painting Pattern

Left Side
Reverse and repeat
for right side

Painted Peacock Jeans

Painted peacocks on the back pockets of these jeans are accented with metallic iron-on studs. These jeans can be hand-washed.

Designed by Kirsten Jones

SUPPLIES

Jeans
Iron-on metallic studs:
    Gold
    Silver
    Blue
Brush-on fabric paints:
    White
    Light red oxide
    Medium green, teal
    Yellow ochre
    Azure blue
Tracing paper
Transfer paper

TOOLS

#3 round paint brush
Iron
Stylus
Pencil

Pattern
Enlarge @170% for actual size.

INSTRUCTIONS

1. Trace the pattern. Enlarge as needed. Transfer the design to each pocket.
2. Paint the bird, using the photo as a guide for color placement. Let dry.
3. Apply studs: gold around the edges of the pockets, silver for the birds' eyes, and blue for the tail feathers. Follow the package instructions. ❏

Painted Paisley Purse

A soft zipper-top denim purse gets a one-of-a-kind treatment with paints and stud-and-jewel paisley iron-ons. The purse can be hand-washed.

Designed by Kirsten Jones

SUPPLIES

Denim purse

Iron-on studs and jewels, Paisley design

Brush-on fabric paints:

    White

    Coastal blue

    Lavender

    Vintage orange

    Sugar plum

    Autumn leaves

    Fuchsia

    Red violet

    Teal

    Azure blue

Bridal tulle

Tracing paper

TOOLS

Iron

Flat paint brushes – #8, #12

Black marker

White chalk

INSTRUCTIONS

1. Trace the pattern. Enlarge as needed. Transfer the design to your purse. See "Transferring Patterns" for instructions.
2. Paint the paisley designs, using the project photo as a guide for color placement. Add highlights by picking up white paint on the brush, then brush lightly and loosely over the wet paint, blending a little of base color. Let dry.
3. Apply paisley stud outlines inside the painted designs, following the package instructions.
4. Apply the flower design studs around the paisley motifs as shown. ❑

Pattern for Purse
Actual Size

Other Embellishments

Ribbons, ruffles, fur, rubber stamps, and oversized buttons are but a few of the other types of embellishments that can be used on jeans and denim and combined with other techniques to create interesting, one-of-a-kind effects.

Rainbow Ruffles Jeans

Sumptuous satin ribbons in the colors of the rainbow are gathered to make ruffled accents for leg vents and pockets. Stamped golden swirls and randomly rubbed gold paint add some shine.

Designed by Patty Cox

Pictured on page 81.

SUPPLIES

Jeans

Satin ribbon, 7/8" wide:

    18" purple

    27" blue

    33" green

    1 yd. yellow

    1-1/2 yds. orange,

    2 yds. red

Denim scrap that matches jeans, 5" x 10"

Washable permanent fabric glue (fabric bond)

Blue bias tape

Acrylic craft paint, metallic gold

Textile medium

Foam pad, 1/4" thick (to use as a stamp pad)

Sewing thread to match ribbon colors

TOOLS

Rubber stamp – Swirl motif

Sewing machine

Scissors

Iron

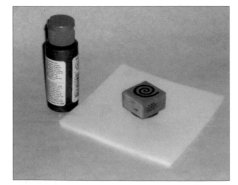

INSTRUCTIONS

Ankle Ruffles:

1. Cut away 1/2" x 5" of the outer side seam at each ankle. Zig-zag over cut edges. Turn edges under 1/4". Zig-zag over turned edge.
2. Sew a long basting stitch 1/8" from one long edge of the purple ribbon. Pull threads to gather. Starting 1" from the end of the ribbon, place the gathered edge of the ribbon along the turned edge of the denim, with the ruffle facing out. Sew the ribbon to the denim over the gathers.
3. Gather blue ribbon 1/8" from edge. Place the blue ribbon so it overlaps the gathered edge of the purple ruffle 1/2". Sew gathered edge of blue ruffle to jeans.
4. Gather and sew the green ribbon, then the yellow, then orange, then red.
5. Turn the ends of the ribbon over the jeans hem and glue inside the jeans. Let dry.
6. Sew or glue bias tape over the ribbon ends. Let dry (if you used glue).

Pocket Ruffles:

1. Cut two 6" lengths of red ribbon and gather 1/8" from each long edge. Gather each ribbon.
2. Sew or glue gathered edges of ribbon to inside top edges of back pockets.

Small Pockets:

1. Cut two small pockets, using the pattern provided.
2. Fold under edges along fold lines. Press.
3. Topstitch along folded edge and 1/4" in from folded edge.
4. Sew or glue pocket bottom and sides above ribbon rainbows on legs.

Stamping & Painting:

1. Mix equal amounts textile medium and gold paint. (You'll only need about 1/2 teaspoon in all.) Place the paint and medium mixture on the foam pad.
2. Press the rubber stamp on the foam, then randomly on the jeans.
3. When you've finished stamping the swirl designs, use the foam pad to rub gold paint across the seams of the jeans, along the edges of the pockets, and randomly on areas of the legs. ❑

Pictured at left: The paint, the stamp, the foam pad.

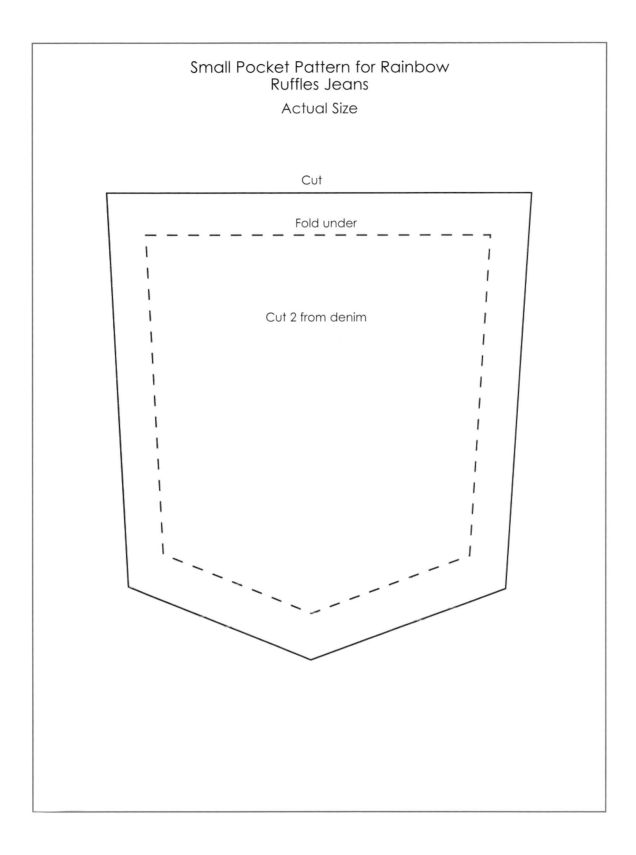

Small Pocket Pattern for Rainbow
Ruffles Jeans

Actual Size

Cut

Fold under

Cut 2 from denim

Fur & Rhinestone-Trimmed Jeans Jacket

A fur collar and cuffs – genuine or faux – adds a luxurious look to a plain jeans jacket. Two collar options are provided – one that matches the size of the jacket's denim collar; the other is larger and uses more of the rabbit skin.

Designed by Patty Cox

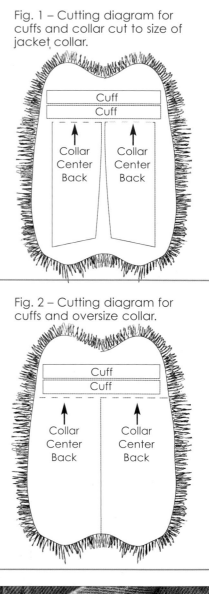

Fig. 1 – Cutting diagram for cuffs and collar cut to size of jacket collar.

Fig. 2 – Cutting diagram for cuffs and oversize collar.

SUPPLIES

Jeans jacket

Rabbit fur skin *or* 1/2 yd. faux fur

1/3 yd. black lining fabric

10 sew-on snaps, 21mm

10 oversized rhinestone buttons *or* brooches

Washable permanent fabric glue (fabric bond)

Sewing thread

Tracing paper

TOOLS

Craft knife

Sewing needle

Pencil

INSTRUCTIONS

1. Buttons or snaps on the jacket can be removed or left in place. Sew one-half of a 21mm snap over each button or snap (or in the place where the button was). Sew the other half of the snap under the buttonhole. (Photo 1)

2. Open jacket and place on a flat surface. Trace around jacket collar and cuff on tracing paper. Cut out paper patterns. Arrange patterns on rabbit skin or faux fur. The fur collar can be cut to the same size as the jacket collar (Fig. 1) or widened to use the entire lower portion of the skin (Fig. 2).

3. Cut the fur on the skin side, using a craft knife to cut only through the skin – don't cut the fur.

4. With fur sides facing, hold collar with center back edges together. Whip-stitch the center back seam of the collar. (Photo 2) Knot thread. Use a needle to pull the fur out of the seam.

5. Pin the pattern pieces on the lining fabric, placing the collar to make one continuous piece.

6. Place lining, right side out, next to skin. Zig-zag stitch (6 to 8 stitches per inch) around the skin and lining edges, moving the fur out of the way as you stitch. Use a sewing needle to pull out any fur that got caught in the thread.

7. Use the same procedure to sew the cuff lining pieces to the fur cuffs.

8. Sew collar and cuffs to jacket, using long running stitches (2 stitches per inch). *Option:* Use snaps or hooks and eyes to attach the lining side of the fur pieces to the jacket.

9. Pin brooches in place or sew oversized buttons over the jacket buttonholes. ❑

Photo 1 – Snaps sewn in place.

Photo 2 – Center back seam of collar whip-stitched.

84

jeans Makeovers

Jeans that don't fit or that become damaged or outdated can be recycled to create new clothes and home decor objects. Recycling is also a great way to use those jeans that are a sentimental favorite; thrift stores and secondhand clothing stores are other sources of used jeans.

You can use pieces of jeans or jeans skirts, for example, to make a skirt bottom or to add new legs to jeans. You can also use parts of jeans to make all manner of fun purses, pouches, and tote bags. This section also includes ideas for using jeans to make aprons, pillows, and a cover for a journal with handmade denim paper.

SWIRL SKIRT

Instructions appear on page 88.

Swirl Skirt

This skirt starts with the top from a pair of jeans. The swirl pattern can be adapted to fit any size jeans. An embroidered paisley accent echoes the shape of the swirl.

Designed by Patty Cox

Pictured on page 87.

SUPPLIES

3 to 4 pairs of jeans (light, medium, and dark values)

Sewing thread

Embroidery floss:

Dark red

Red

Yellow gold

Bright green

Tracing paper

Transfer paper

TOOLS

Sewing machine

Scissors

Pencil

Stylus

Embroidery hoop

Iron

INSTRUCTIONS

Cut:

1. Cut top (approximately) 10" from a pair of jeans that fit well in the waist and hips. This cut should include the back pockets and be 1-1/2" below the back pockets. Take care not to cut through the front pockets.
2. Measure the distance around the bottom of the cut-off jeans top.
3. Trace the swirl skirt pattern piece. Enlarge as directed. To adjust the pattern to fit your jeans top, measure the top of the swirl pattern piece, multiply by 6 (the number of pieces), and subtract 1-1/2" (1/4" seam allowance on all pieces).
4. Compare the numbers – they need to be the same. If they are not, increase or decrease the width of the pattern as needed.
5. Determine how long you want the skirt to be. Measure the length of the jeans top and the length of the swirl pattern piece. Add the two measurements and compare to desired length. Increase or decrease swirl pattern piece as needed.
6. Make a pattern piece that fits your measurement decisions.
7. Cut two light, two medium, and two dark denim sections, following the seam placement line on the pattern piece.

Sew:

1. With right sides facing, sew sections together, using a 1/4" seam allowance. Press all seams to one side, all in the same direction. *Option:* Topstitch side seams.
2. Turn jeans top inside out. Pin bottom edge to skirt top. Sew the bottom of the jeans top to the top of the skirt, using a 1/4" seam allowance. Turn right side out. Press seam up. Topstitch over seam.
3. Zig-zag stitch along the scalloped edge of the skirt hem to prevent fraying. Machine straight stitch along the hem 1/2" from the bottom. Turn up hem along stitched edge. Press.
4. Topstitch 1/8" from the turned scalloped edge. Sew a second row of topstitching 3/8" from the turned edge.

Embroider:

1. Trace paisley pattern and transfer to skirt under front pocket.
2. Center design in embroidery hoop. Satin stitch the paisley design, using three strands of embroidery floss. Use the photo and the pattern as guides for color placement. ❏

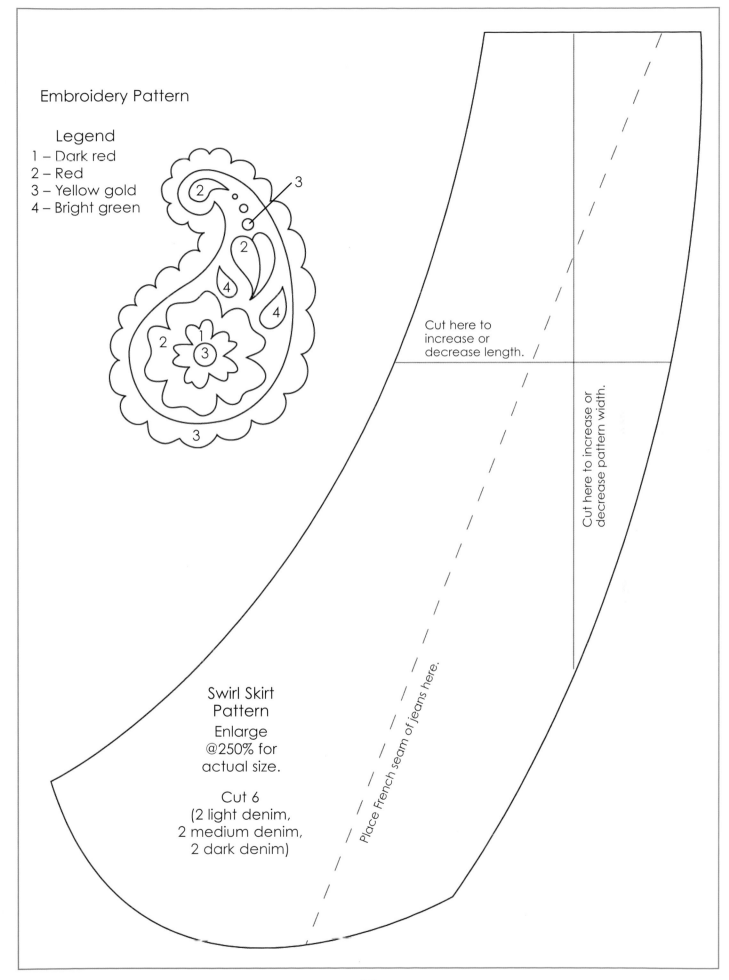

Embroidery Pattern

Legend
1 – Dark red
2 – Red
3 – Yellow gold
4 – Bright green

Cut here to increase or decrease length.

Cut here to increase or decrease pattern width.

Place French seam of jeans here.

Swirl Skirt Pattern
Enlarge @250% for actual size.

Cut 6
(2 light denim,
2 medium denim,
2 dark denim)

Swirl Flare Jeans

A swirl pattern adds flair (and flare!) to the bottoms of the legs of these jeans. They are decorated with heart-shaped iron-on appliques and embroidered accents.

Designed by Patty Cox

SUPPLIES

Knee-length (or longer) jeans (to use for the top)

3 pairs of jeans, light, medium, and dark values (to use for the swirl bottoms)

Fusible web

Sewing thread

Embroidery floss:

Yellow gold

Red

Green

Turquoise

Optional: Liquid fray preventative

TOOLS

Sewing machine

Embroidery needle

Scissors

Iron

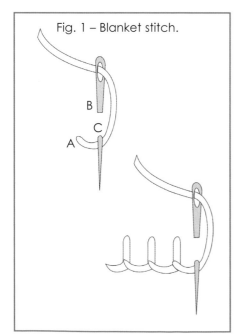

Fig. 1 – Blanket stitch.

INSTRUCTIONS

Cut:

1. Cut lower legs from jeans approximately 14" above the hem (below the knee).
2. Measure the distance around the bottom of the cut-off jeans legs.
3. Trace the swirl pattern piece. Enlarge as directed. To adjust the pattern to fit your jeans, measure the top of the swirl pattern piece, multiply by 6 (the number of pieces), and subtract 1-1/2" (1/4" seam allowance on all pieces).
4. Compare the numbers – they need to be the same. If they are not, increase or decrease the width of the pattern as needed.
5. Increase or decrease the length of the pattern piece as needed, allowing for a 3/8" hem.
6. Cut two light, two medium, and two dark denim sections. Set aside.
7. Reverse the pattern. Cut two of each color of denim.

Sew:

1. To make one leg bottom, with right sides facing, sew the sides of one set of six pieces together, using a 1/4" seam allowance. Press seams to one side, all going in the same direction.
2. Repeat step 1, using the other set of leg pieces.
3. Zig-zag stitch the scalloped edge of each leg bottom piece. Machine straight stitch 3/8" from scalloped edges. Turn up hem along stitched edge. Press. Hand or machine topstitch the hem.
4. Determine which leg bottom belongs on which leg. (The swirls should turn out when attached.) Turn flared leg bottoms inside out.
5. Slide the flared bottom over the appropriate jeans leg with the top of the pieced section even with the cut edge of the jeans leg. Pin in place. Sew flare to jeans leg, using a 1/4" seam allowance. Turn right side out. Press seam down.
6. Repeat step 5 to attach the remaining flared bottom.

Heart Patches:

1. Iron fusible web to the wrong sides of the denim scraps. Using the patterns provided, cut out denim hearts.
2. Position and iron heart patches on jeans, using the photo as a guide. **Option:** Apply fray preventative around the edges of each heart. Let dry.

Embroidery:

1. Thread an embroidery needle with 3-ply embroidery floss. Blanket stitch around each heart patch.
2. Blanket stitch along pocket edges and waist. ❏

Pattern appears on page 92.

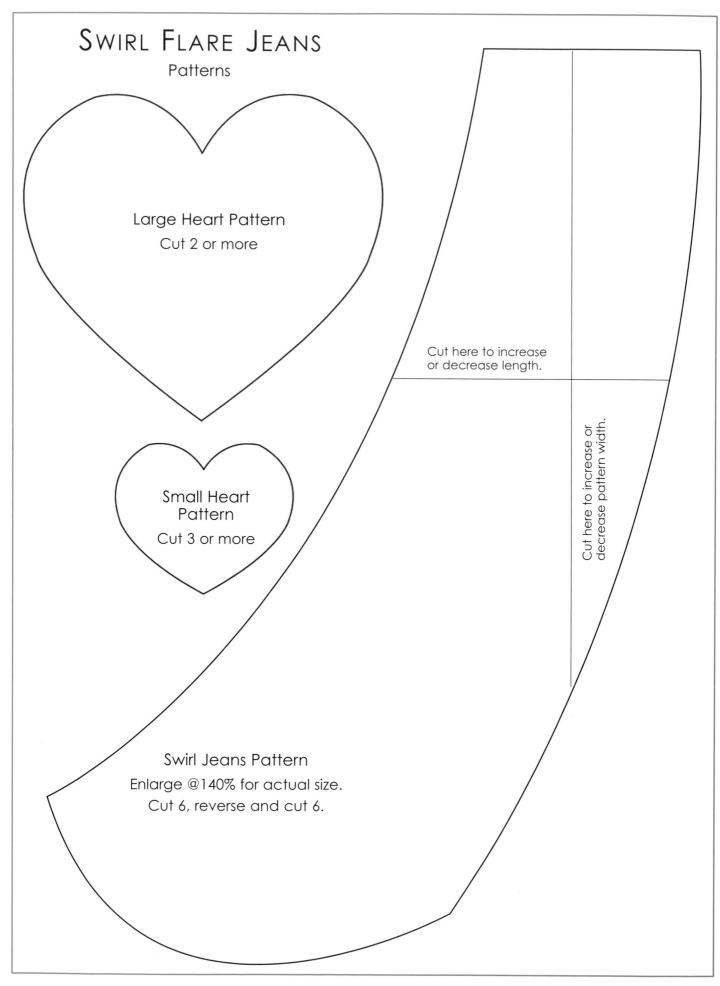

SWIRL FLARE JEANS

Patterns

Large Heart Pattern
Cut 2 or more

Small Heart
Pattern
Cut 3 or more

Cut here to increase
or decrease length.

Cut here to increase or
decrease pattern width.

Swirl Jeans Pattern
Enlarge @140% for actual size.
Cut 6, reverse and cut 6.

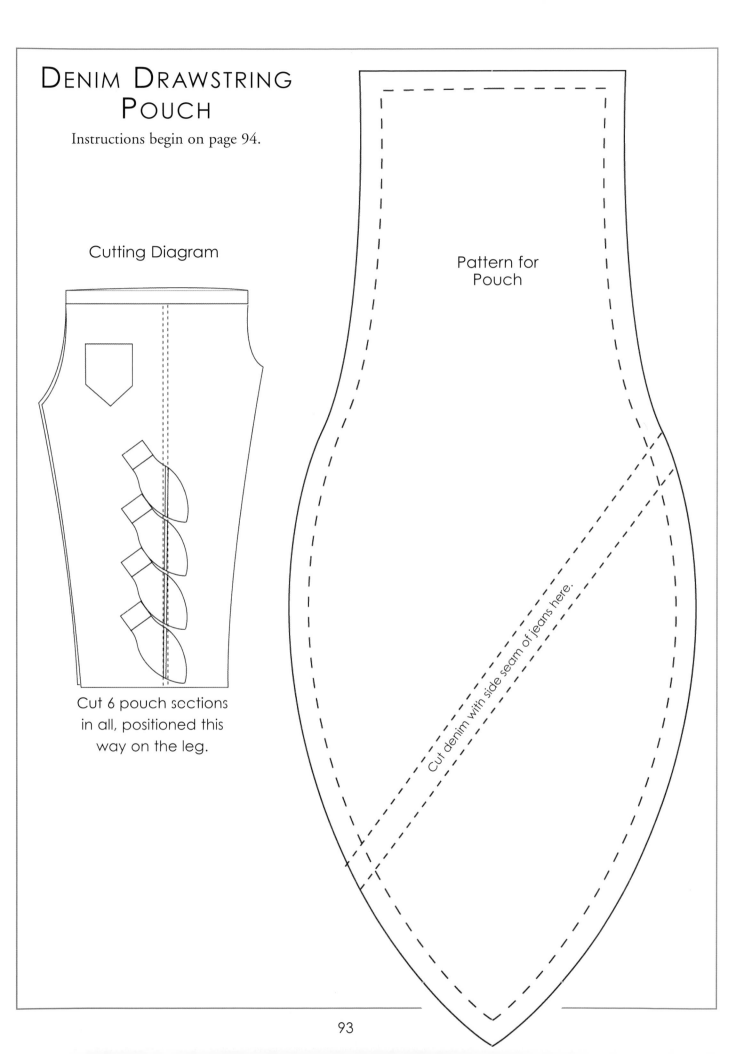

Denim Drawstring Pouch

Instructions begin on page 94.

Cutting Diagram

Cut 6 pouch sections
in all, positioned this
way on the leg.

Pattern for
Pouch

Cut denim with side seam of jeans here.

Denim Drawstring Pouch

Silky-looking cording and tassels from the drapery section of the fabric story accent this denim pouch. Belt loops removed from jeans hold the drawstring in place.

Designed by Patty Cox

See page 98 for pattern.

SUPPLIES

Jeans

3 belt loops from jeans

Gold tassel, 3-1/2"

26" gold cord with 3" tassels at ends

1/3 yd. fabric (for lining)

Sewing thread

Lightweight cardboard

Fabric marker

Tracing paper

Transfer paper

Fabric marker

TOOLS

Sewing machine

Scissors

Pencil

Stylus

Craft knife

Cutting mat

Iron

INSTRUCTIONS

Cut:

1. Trace pattern. Transfer to cardboard. Cut out cardboard to make a template, using a craft knife.
2. Using the cutting diagram on the previous page as a guide, trace around the template to make six denim purse sections, placing the seam of the jeans leg on the diagonal as shown. Cut out.
3. Using the same template, cut six sections of lining fabric.

Sew:

1. Sew the denim pieces together along the sides, using a 1/4" seam allowance. Before sewing the last seam, insert the 3-1/2" gold tassel at the bottom point of the pouch. Sew that seam, catching the top end of the tassel in the seam. Press seams.
2. Sew the six lining pieces together. Press.
3. Turn pouch right side out. Turn lining inside out. Place the lining inside the pouch, aligning the seams.
4. Turn under the top raw edge of both bag and lining 1/4". Press. Topstitch around the top of the pouch.
5. Cut belt loops in half. Turn under raw edge. Position the six shortened belt loops around the top of the pouch, one at each seam. Stitch top and bottom ends of loops securely.
6. Thread the 26" gold cord with tassels through the belt loops to make a drawstring and shoulder strap. Knot tassel ends together. ❑

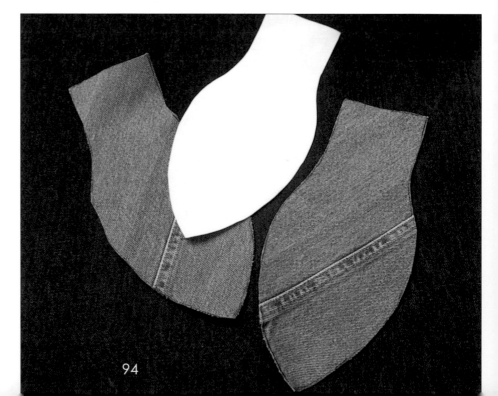

Pictured at right: Template made from pattern and two cut pieces.

Jeans Bib Apron

The back yoke and back pockets section of a child's pair of jeans provide a sturdy bib for a chef's apron. The rest of the apron is cut from a playful lobster-patterned canvas print and embellished with pockets made from the bottom part of the jean's legs.

Designed by Patty Cox

SUPPLIES

Child's size 12 jeans (for apron top and pockets)

3/4 yd. print canvas or other sturdy fabric

2-1/4 yds. red cording

Blue bias tape, 1/2" wide

Sewing thread

Tracing paper

TOOLS

Sewing machine

Scissors

Iron

Pencil

INSTRUCTIONS

Apron Top & Bottom:

See Fig. 1.

1. Cut off top back of jeans 10" from waistband, about 1" below the bottoms of the back pockets. Cut away side seams so the bottom of the denim piece is 20-1/2" wide.

2. Cut a 20" x 26" piece of your selected print fabric. Turn under bottom and side raw edges 1/2". Press. Turn under 1/2" again. Press. Topstitch.

3. Sew jeans piece of canvas piece, letting jeans piece extend 1/4" beyond each side of the canvas piece. Zig-zag over raw edges to finish seam. Press seam down. Topstitch over seam.

Pockets:

1. Trace pocket pattern and cut out.

2. Cut two denim pockets from the jeans legs, placing the pattern so the hemmed edge is the pocket top. Turn side and bottom edges under 1/2". Press.

3. Position pockets on apron, using Fig. 1 as a guide. Topstitch in place.

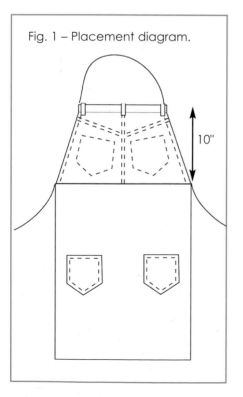

Fig. 1 – Placement diagram.

10"

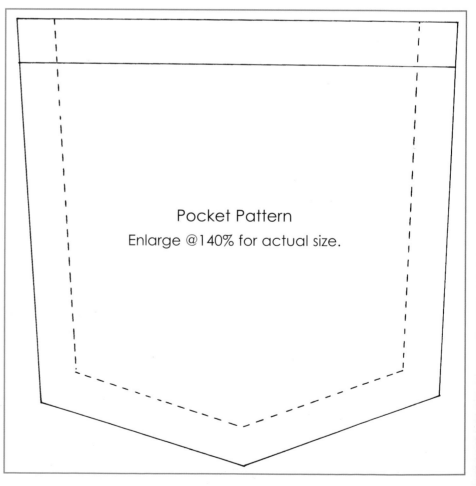

Pocket Pattern
Enlarge @140% for actual size.

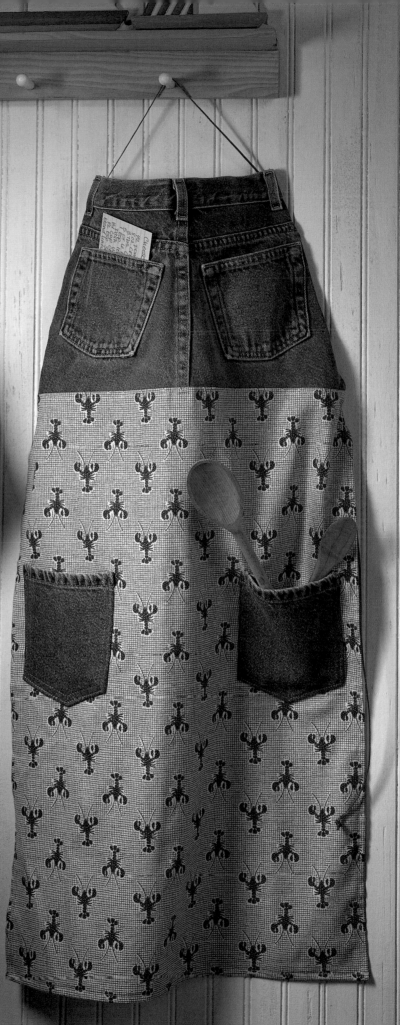

Drawstring:

1. Cut two pieces of bias tape, each 11" long. Open folded edges and turn under cut ends 1/4". Press. Turn again 1/4". Press. Stitch to hem the ends of both pieces.

2. With right sides facing, sew bias tape to each side of apron top, using a 1/4" seam allowance and leaving the hemmed ends open. Press tape to back.

3. Topstitch the edge of the tape to the wrong side of the apron top, forming a casing for the cord.

4. Thread cord from one side of the apron, through the casing. Leave a loop at the top and thread through the casing on the other side. Tie knots in cord ends. ❏

Painted Chef's Apron

Here's a fun idea for recycling a pair of jeans. It would be a great gift for a lobster lover. The lobster and lemon designs are painted onto the apron.

Designed by Patty Cox

SUPPLIES

Jeans
2-1/4 yds. red cording
Navy blue bias tape, 1/2" wide, 7/8" wide
Red jumbo rick rack
Sewing thread
Acrylic craft paints:
    Pale yellow
    Bright yellow
    Lime green
Textile medium
Dimensional tube paint, Red shiny
Permanent black marking pen
Tracing paper
Transfer paper

TOOLS

Sewing machine
Iron
Scissors
Paint brushes
Pencil
Stylus

INSTRUCTIONS

See Fig. 1 for dimensions and assembly.
Apron Bib:
1. Cut the top back of a pair of jeans 11-1/2" from the waistband (about 1" below the back pockets) to create the bib. Cut away the side seams.
2. To remove the fullness at the crotch seam so the bib will lay flat, open the flat-felled crotch seam and allow the two sides to overlap until they lay flat on your work surface and the piece on top curves over the piece on the bottom.
3. Topstitch over the curved seam to secure. (Fig. 2)

Apron Bottom:

1. Cut off 22" of the upper thighs of the jeans. Open each leg at the outer seam.
2. Place legs together, right sides facing. Sew the two leg pieces together at center front with a flat-felled seam. (Fig. 3)
3. With right sides together, sew apron bib to apron bottom. Zig-zag to finish the seam. Press seam flat toward the top.
4. Topstitch over seam.
5. Using Fig. 1 as a guide, cut curves at waist about 2" deep and 4" wide. Round the lower side corners of the apron.

Pockets:

1. Cut denim pockets from left-over jeans fabric, making the hemmed edge of the leg the top of the pocket. Cut pockets 9" wide x 8" deep with a point at center bottom. Press sides under 1".
2. Position pockets on apron. Topstitch in place.

3. With right sides facing, sew the 7/8" bias tape to the raw edges of the apron bib and the waist curves. Turn the tape to the back. Press. Topstitch or hand-stitch the tape to the back, forming a casing for the cord.
4. Thread cording from one apron waist side to neck. Thread down other casing from neck to waist side. Tie knots in cord ends.

Painting:

1. Trace pattern and transfer to apron.
2. Paint lobsters with shiny dimensional paint.
3. Mix textile medium with acrylic paints according to the package instructions.
4. Paint lemon slices with pale yellow.
5. Paint whole lemons with bright yellow.
6. Paint swirls with lime green. Let dry.
7. Outline lemons and add details to slices with black pen.
8. Squeeze dots of red dimensional paint around the painted design, using the pattern as a guide. ❑

Painting Pattern
Enlarge @245% for actual size.

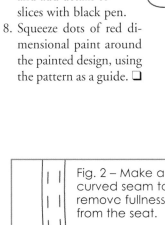

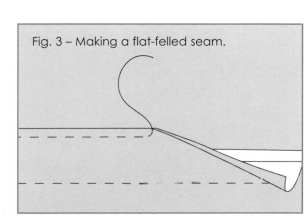

Fig. 1 – Assembly diagram.

14"

11½"

4"

2"

9" x 8"

22"

42"

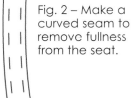

Fig. 2 – Make a curved seam to remove fullness from the seat.

Edge Finishing:

1. With right sides facing, sew 1/2" bias tape to raw edges of the sides of the apron bottom (but not the curved upper areas). Turn tape to back. Press. Topstitch on the edge to secure.
2. Cut two pieces of 7/8" bias tape to fit the apron from the top to the sides (including the curves) plus 1". Open the folded edges of the bias tape and turn under cut ends 1/4". Press. Turn again 1/4". Press. Stitch to hem the ends of each piece.

Fig. 3 – Making a flat-felled seam.

Tooth Fairy Pillow

Children will love this denim tooth fairy doll with an embroidered face and curly yarn hair. Stuffed canvas garden gloves make fanciful wings, and an embroidered jeans pocket holds teeth, money, or tokens.

Designed by Patty Cox

SUPPLIES

Jeans leg

1 pr. canvas gloves (for wings)

1/4 yd. canvas (same color as gloves, for head)

Embroidery floss:

    Dark blue

    White

    Yellow

    Rust

    Dark red

Polyester stuffing

1 yd. blue cord

4 round wooden beads, 10mm

4 round wooden beads, 20mm

4 ecru crocheted doilies, 1-1/2"

1 crocheted doily, 4"

Washable permanent fabric glue (fabric bond)

Yarn – Terra cotta (for the hair)

Sewing thread

Cardboard, 3" x 6"

TOOLS

Sewing machine

Scissors

Fabric marker

Awl

Sewing needle

Iron

INSTRUCTIONS

Body:

1. Cut an 8-1/2" long section about 9" wide from the jeans leg. (Fig. 1)
2. With right sides of denim together, sew a 1/4" seam along one 9" edge. (Fig. 2)
3. Open corners. Align bottom seam and side seam. Measure 1-1/2" in from point. (Fig. 3) Draw a line perpendicular to the seam. Sew on the line. Repeat for other side. Turn right side out.

Arms & Legs:

1. Cut two 7" lengths of blue cord for arms. Cut two 11" lengths of blue cord for legs. Tie a knot in each cord end.
2. Use an awl to puncture small holes in the denim body at arm and leg placement areas. Insert the cords (shorter ones for arms, longer ones for legs) from inside the body through the holes, with the knots inside. Secure knots inside the body with fabric glue.
3. Thread a 1-1/2" ecru crocheted doily over each cord. Glue each doily to the denim body.
4. Thread a 10mm wooden bead, then a 20mm wooden bead on each cord as "hands" and "feet." Knot each cord end. Secure beads in place with a dot of fabric glue on cord under each bead.

Continued on page 102

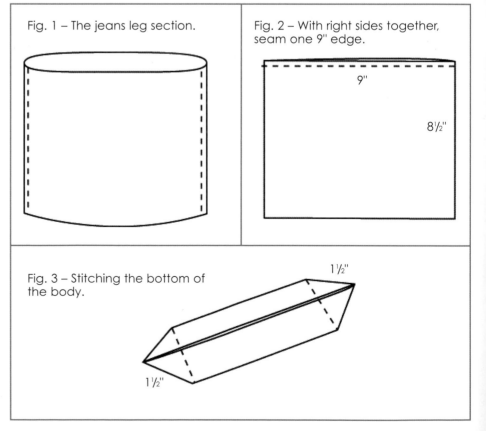

Fig. 1 – The jeans leg section.

Fig. 2 – With right sides together, seam one 9" edge.

9"

8½"

Fig. 3 – Stitching the bottom of the body.

1½"

1½"

Tooth Fairy Pillow

continued from page 100

5. Fill body with stuffing. Hand sew a running stitch around the open top edge. Pull tightly to gather. Knot thread. Clip ends.

6. Glue the 4" crocheted doily over the gathers to make a collar for the doll.

Head:

1. Cut an 8" x 5" piece of canvas. (Fig. 4)

2. Fold in half. (Fig. 5) Sew 1/4" seam along the long side and across one 4" end.

3. Open corners. Align bottom seam and side seam. Measure 1/2" in from the point. Draw a line perpendicular to the seam. (Fig. 6) Sew on line. Repeat for other side. Turn right side out.

4. Using the pattern provided, embroider the face details on the front of the head. Use the stem stitch for the nose and mouth lines (Stitching Diagram 1) and French knots (Stitching Diagram 3) for the eyes.

5. Stuff the head. Hand sew running stitches to gather the open edge. Pull gathers tightly. Knot thread. Clip ends.

Hair:

1. Cut out 1/4" x 2" section from the center of the piece of cardboard. (Fig. 7)

2. Wrap yarn around the cardboard end. (Fig. 8) Machine stitch over the center of the wraps through the cutout in the cardboard. Slide the stitched wraps off the card.

3. Wrap and sew another section of loops. Continue stitching until you have made 36" of wrapped loops.

4. Fold loops in half along center seam. Glue loops around head starting at the bottom (Fig. 9) and continuing up the sides and around the top. (Fig. 10)

5. Glue the head to the top of the body.

Pocket:

1. Using the pattern provided, cut out a denim pocket. Turn and press raw edges under on the fold lines. Topstitch along the lines on the pattern to hem.

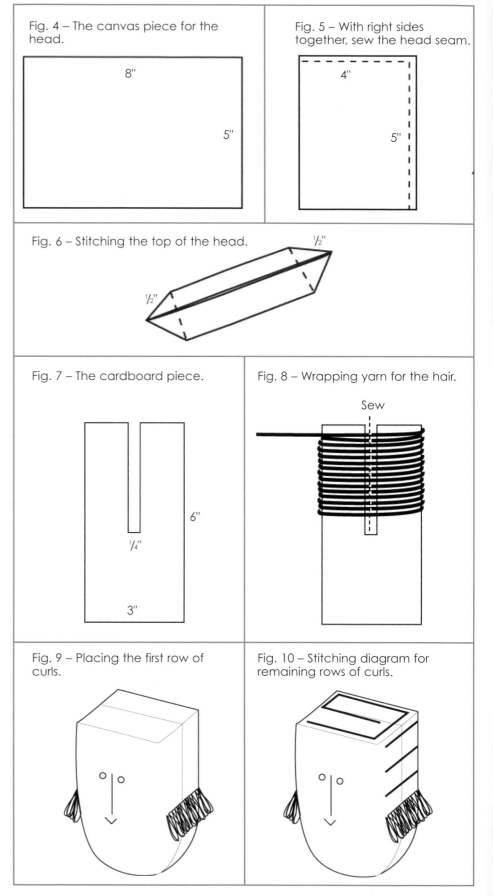

Fig. 4 – The canvas piece for the head.

Fig. 5 – With right sides together, sew the head seam.

Fig. 6 – Stitching the top of the head.

Fig. 7 – The cardboard piece.

Fig. 8 – Wrapping yarn for the hair.

Fig. 9 – Placing the first row of curls.

Fig. 10 – Stitching diagram for remaining rows of curls.

2. Stem stitch the "tooth fairy" lettering (Stitching Diagram 1) using six strands dark blue embroidery floss.

3. Dot the "i" with a yellow French knot. (Stitching Diagram 3)

4. Embroider five lazy daisy stitches around the French knot. (Stitching Diagram 4)

5. Blanket stitch around the edges of the pocket with six strands rust embroidery floss. (Stitching Diagram 2)

6. Glue the pocket sides and bottom to the front of the doll body.

Wings:

1. Fold the knitted cuffs to the inside of each glove. Lightly stuff each glove.

2. Place the open end of one glove end inside the other glove, overlapping 1". Whipstitch gloves together to make the wings.

3. Sew a running stitch through the wings' center. Pull stitches tightly to gather. Tie off thread. Cut thread ends.

4. Sew and glue wings on the back of the upper body. ❑

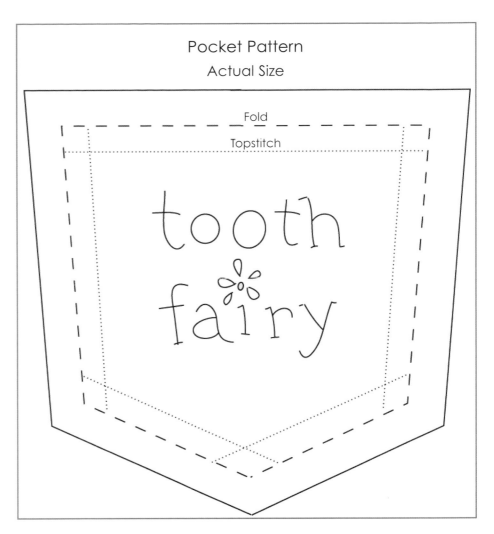

Pocket Pattern
Actual Size

Fold

Topstitch

tooth fairy

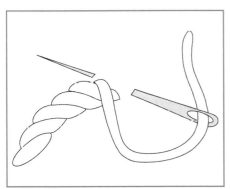

Diagram 1 – Stem stich

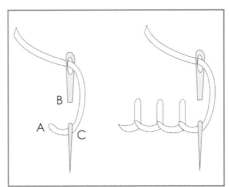

Diagram 2 – Blanket stitch

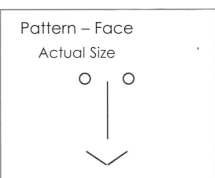

Pattern – Face
Actual Size

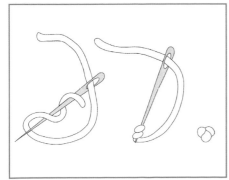

Diagram 3 – French Knot

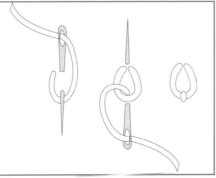

Diagram 4 – Lazy Daisy

Denim Diaper Duffel

What a great gift for a new mom or a mom-to-be! It is heavy duty and very durable.

Designed by Patty Cox

SUPPLIES

2 to 3 pairs of jeans

1-1/2 yds. fabric (for lining)

2 D-rings, 2"

Elastic, 3/8" wide and 1/2" wide

1-1/3 yds. navy blue webbing, 2" wide

4 navy blue buttons, 1-1/4"

Sewing thread

Optional: Black elastic cord

TOOLS

Scissors

Sewing machine

Iron

Large safety pin

INSTRUCTIONS

Bag:

1. Cut open side seams open of one pair of jeans. Cut two 24" lengths from legs. (Fig. 1)
2. Cut two pieces the same size from lining fabric. Set aside.
3. With right sides of denim together, sew 1/2" seams along the bag sides and bottom.
4. Press open bottom seam. Align bottom seam with side seam. Mark 3" in from each point. Machine straight stitch across point. (Fig. 2)
5. Repeat steps 3 and 4 with the lining fabric to construct the lining. Set aside.
6. To sew the casing, fold top 1/4" raw edge of denim bag to inside. Machine straight stitch over turned edge. Fold edge of bag to inside 1". Machine straight stitch casing 1/8" from edge, leaving a small opening. (Fig. 3)
7. Place the lining inside the bag. Turn under the top raw edge of the lining, aligning the folded edge with the lower edge of the casing. Hand or machine stitch the top of the lining inside the denim bag.
8. Cut a 17" piece of 1/2" elastic. Attach a large safety pin to one end. Thread elastic through the top casing. (Fig. 4) Remove the pin.
9. Machine stitch elastic ends together securely. Stitch casing opening closed.
10. To make the handle, cut two 3" lengths of webbing. Fold each over a D-ring. Place the D-rings on opposite sides of the bag with the webbing overlapping the casing. (Fig. 5) Sew webbing inside bag.

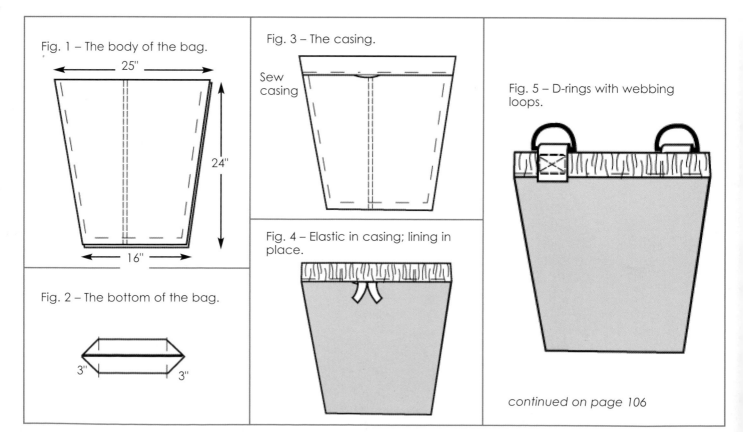

Fig. 1 – The body of the bag.

25"

24"

16"

Fig. 2 – The bottom of the bag.

3"   3"

Fig. 3 – The casing.

Sew casing

Fig. 4 – Elastic in casing; lining in place.

Fig. 5 – D-rings with webbing loops.

continued on page 106

DENIM DIAPER DUFFEL

continued from page 104

Pockets:

1. Cut four 10" tall sections from the lower leg areas of the jeans. (Fig. 6)

2. Place each jeans section on lining fabric. Cut two lining pieces for each jeans section that are 1/2" larger all around than the jeans section. (Fig. 7)

3. With right sides facing, sew lining side seams and bottom seam, using a 1/2" seam allowance. (Fig. 8) Repeat for each pocket lining.

4. Turn one leg section wrong side out, centering the French seam. Sew a 1/2" seam along the narrow end. (Fig. 9) Press open the bottom seam. Mark a line 1" in from each corner point. Machine straight stitch across each point. Repeat for each jeans section.

5. To make the pocket casings, fold over the top 1/4" raw edge of the pocket to the inside. Machine straight stitch over turned edge. Fold over edge of pocket to inside 1". Machine straight stitch 1/8" from edge to make a casing, leaving a small opening. (Fig. 10) Repeat on the rest of the pockets.

6. Place one pocket lining inside one pocket. Turn under the top raw edge and press. Align the folded edge with the lower edge of the pocket casing. Hand or machine stitch the lining inside the pocket. Repeat for all pockets.

7. Cut four 12" pieces of 3/8" wide elastic. Attach a large safety pin to the end of one piece. Thread through the top casing of one pocket. (Fig. 11) Remove the pin. Machine stitch elastic ends together securely. Stitch casing opening closed. Repeat the process to add elastic to each pocket casing.

Assembly:

1. Align and center bottom edges of pockets with the bottom edge of the bag. (Fig. 12) Machine sew pocket bottoms to the bag bottom edge, 1/8" from the pocket bottom edges.

2. Working one pocket at a time, pin the top of the pocket to the side of the bag, placing the pocket as shown in Fig. 13.

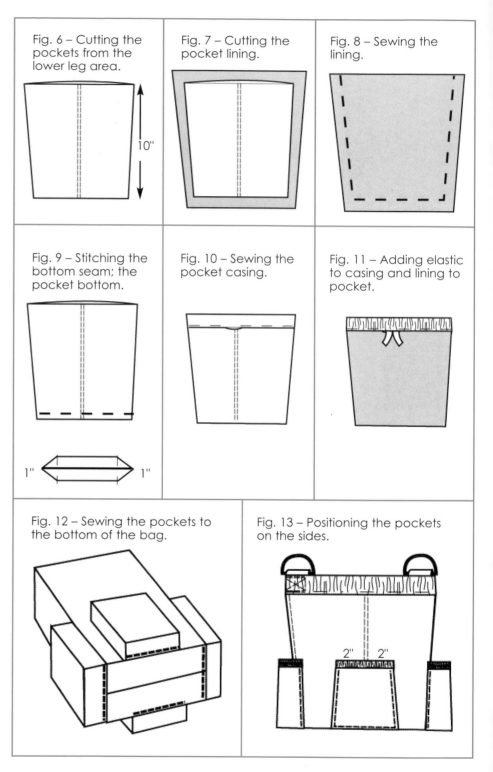

Fig. 6 – Cutting the pockets from the lower leg area.

Fig. 7 – Cutting the pocket lining.

Fig. 8 – Sewing the lining.

Fig. 9 – Stitching the bottom seam; the pocket bottom.

Fig. 10 – Sewing the pocket casing.

Fig. 11 – Adding elastic to casing and lining to pocket.

Fig. 12 – Sewing the pockets to the bottom of the bag.

Fig. 13 – Positioning the pockets on the sides.

Machine sew pocket sides to bag 1/8" from the edge of the pocket. Repeat to sew all four pockets, centering each over the side seams of the bag.

3. Sew a 1-1/4" button at the top center of each pocket. *Option: Sew a loop of elastic cord on the back of the pocket at the top. Loop cord around button to close pocket.*

4. To attach the strap, cut 1 yd. of 2" webbing. Fold 1-1/2" of one end over one D-ring. Sew webbing end securely. Repeat for other end. ❑

Denim Organizer

Use this tall organizer to hold tools on your workbench or as a casual vase for a wild-flower bouquet.

Designed by Patty Cox

SUPPLIES

Child's jeans
46 oz. juice can
Fabric glue
White craft ("tacky") glue
Upholstery thread

TOOLS

Sewing needle
Can opener
Ruler
Fabric marker
Scissors

INSTRUCTIONS

1. Drain contents of juice can into another container. Remove top from can with a can opener. Wash and dry can.
2. Slide open end of can down into jeans leg. Align jeans hem seam along can rim. (The hem will extend and rest above the rim – Fig. 1.) The jeans leg should fit snugly around the can. Take in the side seam of the jeans if an adjustment is needed.
3. Measure and mark jeans leg 1" beyond the bottom of the can. Cut jeans leg on mark. (Fig. 1)
4. Gather denim along cut edge, using a running stitch and upholstery thread. Pull threads tightly. Apply tacky glue under gathered fabric. Adhere gathered denim to the bottom of the can.
5. Cut both pockets from jeans back, leaving topstitching intact and cutting jeans fabric 1/4" above the pocket tops. Trim jeans fabric even with the pockets along the sides and bottom.
6. Fold down the top flap of the fabric behind the pocket toward the back. Glue down. Let dry. Repeat on other pocket.
7. Working one pocket a time, apply fabric glue to fabric on back of pocket. Position one pocket on each side of the denim-covered can and glue in place between side seams. Place other pocket on other side. Let dry. ❏

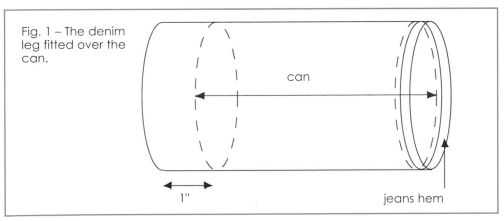

Fig. 1 – The denim leg fitted over the can.

can

1"

jeans hem

107

Cabbage Rose Pillow with Narrow Ruffles

Old pairs of jeans can be cut into strips to create this charming rose ruffled pillow. This is a great gift for a teenager.

Designed by Patty Cox

Pictured on opposite page, bottom.

SUPPLIES

Jeans

Polyester stuffing

Washable permanent fabric glue (fabric bond)

Upholstery thread

TOOLS

Scissors

Sewing needle

Sewing machine

INSTRUCTIONS

Cut:

See Fig. 1 – Cutting Diagram.

1. Cut two denim circles, each 10-1/2" in diameter, from jeans to make pillow front and back.
2. Cut two 1-1/2" strips for a total of 32" in length for the pillow sides. (This piece is called the boxing strip.)
3. Cut 2" wide strips to make the ruffles, using Fig. 1 as a guide.

Sew:

1. Sew the 1-1/2" strips together to make a boxing strip 31" long. Sew the boxing strip to the pillow bottom, using a 1/4" seam allowance.
2. Sew the boxing strip to the pillow top, using a 1/4" seam allowance, leaving a 5" opening.

Make Rose:

1. Fold a 2" denim strip in half lengthwise, right sides out. Gather along the open long edge. Pull gathers and tie off. Note: Gathers don't have to be tight, and the strips do not need to be sewn together end to end.
2. Roll gathered strip unto a tight coil, tucking the raw edges at the ends into the bottom of the coil. Sew or glue the coil at the base. Add another gathered strip around the first, gluing or stitching together. Continue adding strips until cabbage rose is about 10" wide.

Assemble:

1. Glue and sew cabbage rose on the pillow top.
2. Stuff pillow through opening. Sew opening closed. ❏

Fig. 1 – Cutting Diagram

10½"

2" 2" 2" 2" 2" 2" 2"

1½" 1½"

Pictured at right, top to bottom: Cabbage Rose Pillow with Wide Ruffles (instructions appear on page 110), Cabbage Rose Pillow with Narrow Ruffles (instructions appear above). Pillow pattern appears on page 111.

Cabbage Rose Pillow with Wide Ruffle

Designed by Patty Cox

Pictured at top, page 109.

SUPPLIES

3 pairs of jeans *or* 1-1/2 yds. denim

Upholstery thread – Denim blue

Polyester stuffing

Washable permanent fabric glue (fabric bond)

TOOLS

Scissors

Sewing machine

INSTRUCTIONS

Make the Rose:

1. Cut or tear 6" wide denim strips. Sew lengths together, end to end, making a strip 9 feet long and 6" wide. Fold strip, right side out, in half lengthwise. Fold ends under 1/2".

2. Thread needle with upholstery thread. Knot one end. Beginning at one turned end, sew long running stitches through both layers of fabric 1/4" from raw edges for 8". Pull gathering threads tight (Photo 1) and knot, then secure gathers with a second knot. Continue gathering 8" lengths, then knot the thread. Finish gathering the strip, being sure the ends are folded under 1/2". Knot thread.

3. Fold the top corner of one end of the gathered strip down over the bottom corner. (Photo 2) Sew corners together. Coil the turned edge inward. Sew through bottom (gathered) edge of denim layers. (Photo 3) Continue coiling the gathered strip to form the rose, stitching the coil along the bottom edge. (Photo 4)

Photo 1 – Gathering the denim strip with long running stitches.

Photo 2 – Folding over the end to form the center.

Photo 3 – Stitching the gathered strip to coil the rose.

Photo 4 – the bottom of the coiled rose.

Make the Pillow:

1. Cut two 10-1/2" denim circles for the pillow top and bottom.

2. Cut a 2-1/2" x 31" strip for the side of the pillow (the boxing strip).

3. With right sides facing, sew the boxing strip to the edge of the pillow top, using a 1/4" seam allowance. Sew the ends of the boxing strip together.

4. Sew the boxing strip to the pillow bottom, leaving a 4" opening.

5. Stuff the pillow. Hand stitch opening closed.

6. Apply a generous amount of fabric glue to the bottom of the coiled rose and to the bottom of the rose for 2" from the center coil. Center rose on pillow top. Press in place.

7. Hand tack the outer rose petal to the pillow top in five or six places. Let dry. ❑

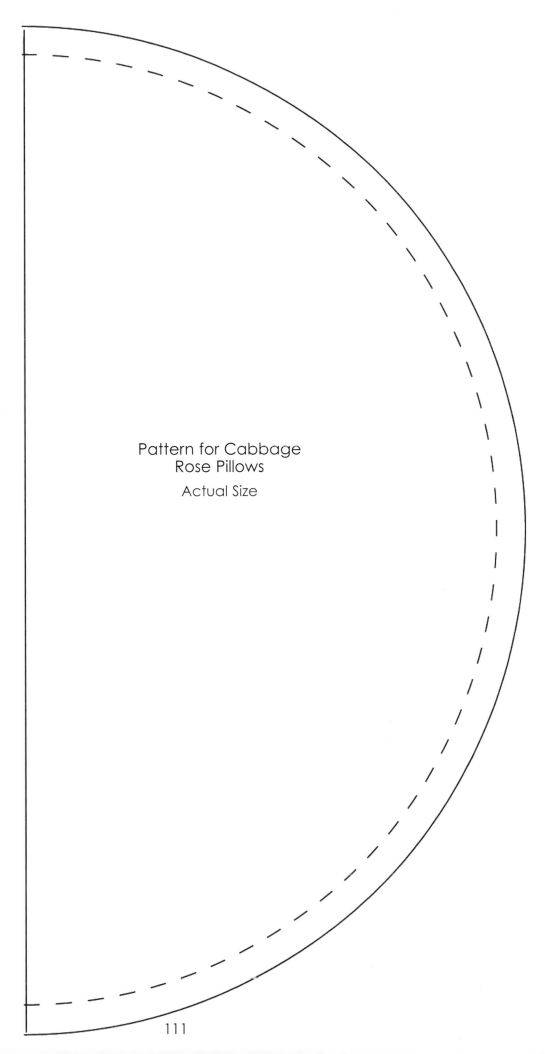

Pattern for Cabbage
Rose Pillows

Actual Size

Jeans Journal

Here's a good way to use those tiny scraps and snippets of denim you accumulate – make it into paper. Yes, the paper is actually made from denim – known as rag paper. Bind the paper inside stiffened denim covers to make a journal or scrapbook.

Designed by Patty Cox

SUPPLIES

For the Cover:

Jeans

3 threaded post screws, 5/8" (also known as binding screws or Chicago screws)

Fabric stiffener liquid

Wax paper

For the Paper:

Denim scraps

Newspaper

10-count plastic needlepoint canvas

Yarn

Pictured at right: The denim paper pages in the journal.
Pictured below: Pieces of denim paper before trimming.

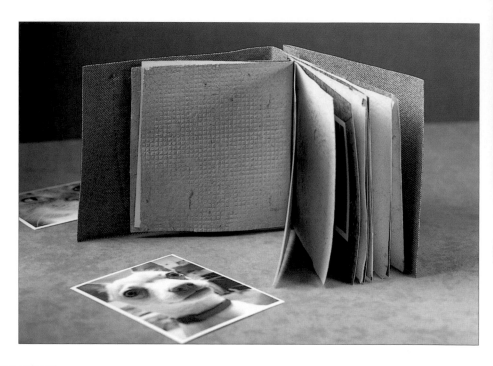

TOOLS

Scissors

Paint brush

1/4" hole punch

Stylus

Ruler

Blender

Bucket

Dishpan

Craft knife

Stapler

Iron

Spray bottle with water

DENIM PAPER INSTRUCTIONS

Prepare:

1. Cut 1/2" square pieces of denim. (Photo 1) Tear newspaper into 2" squares.

2. Fill one-fourth of the bucket with torn pieces of newspaper. Place about 1 cup denim pieces in the bucket. Fill with water. Let soak overnight to loosen all the fibers.

3. Prepare the screens for drying the paper by cutting a rectangle 8-1/4" x 7" from 10-count plastic canvas. Cut squares from each corner that measure 2 holes by 2 holes, and fold up the sides. Whipstitch the corners together with yarn. Knot the yarn to secure. Cut ends. You'll need a screen for each sheet of paper. (Photo 2)

Continued on page 114

JEANS JOURNAL

continued from page 112

Photo 1 – Scraps of denim before soaking.

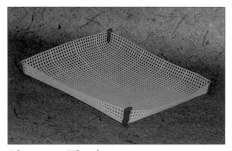

Photo 2 – The drying screen

Photo 3 – Mixing the slurry in a blender.

Photo 4 – Dipping the screen into the slurry.

Blend:

1. Fill the jar of a blender three-fourths full of water. Scoop a handful of the soaked paper-and-denim from the bucket and squeeze into a 1-1/2" to 2" diameter ball. Turn blender with water on medium-high speed. Add paper-and-denim ball and blend about 30 seconds. (Photo 3)

2. Pour the slurry (the paper, denim, and water blend) into a dishpan. Continue blending slurry and adding it to the dishpan until the dishpan is almost full or you've used up all your paper-and-denim mix.

3. Holding the prepared screen at each short end, scoop the screen into the slurry (Photo 4) so the slurry covers the screen. Lift the screen and hold it over the dishpan, allowing the excess water to drip back into the pan. (Photo 5)

4. Place the screen outdoors or in an area where the paper can drip and dry. Allow the paper to dry completely before removing it from screen. The paper will shrink and separate from screen when dry, and will be gray-white in color. (Photo 6)

5. Flatten the paper by spritzing it with water, then pressing it with a hot iron. ❑

COVER INSTRUCTIONS

1. Using the pattern provided, cut two pieces of denim. Cut a pocket from the jeans.

2. Sew or glue the pocket in position on one denim rectangle, using the pattern as a guide.

3. Cover your work surface with wax paper and place the denim on wax paper. Generously coat the denim

Photo 5 – The slurry-covered screen.

Photo 6 – At left, the wet slurry – it's blue – is set out to dry. At right, a dry sheet of paper is gray-white in color.

Photo 7 – Coating the denim pieces with fabric stiffener

pieces with fabric stiffener. (Photo 7) Let dry.

4. Turn denim pieces over and coat other side. Let dry.

5. Trim covers on the cutting lines, using a craft knife.

6. Punch holes with a hole punch. (Fig. 1) Score fold lines with a stylus and ruler. Fold ends to inside. (Fig. 2)

Fig. 1 – Punch holes with paper punch.

fold line

Fig. 2 – Score and fold ends to inside.

Fig. 3 – Place binding screw head under flap.

7. Trim the paper (handmade denim paper or other paper) to fit the journal cover. Punch holes in paper to match holes in covers. Add denim paper to journal.

8. Place one part of the binding screw head under hinged flap. (Fig. 3) Place the other part of the binding screw under the other hinged flap. Place all three screws in holes. Add journal paper on screw posts. Screw posts together to secure. ❏

Pattern for Journal Cover
Actual Size

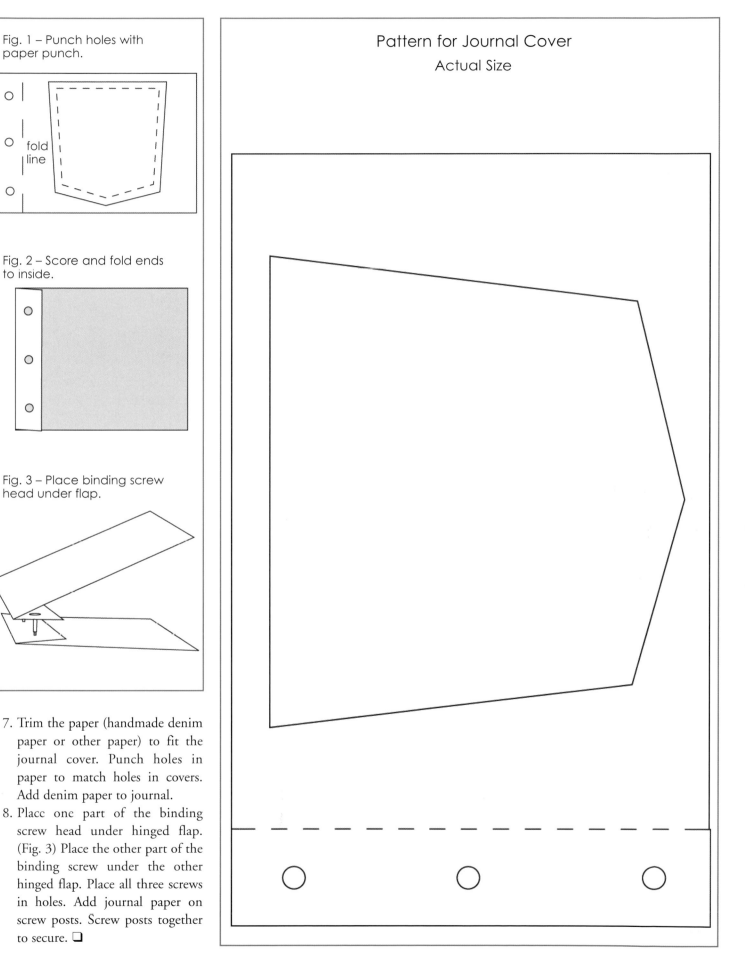

Belted Jeans Bag

Designed by Patty Cox

Here's a wonderful way to use a favorite belt – one from that outfit you no longer wear, or one that's too small. It's the perfect finishing touch for this jeans top bag. Color coordinate the embroidery to match your belt.

116

SUPPLIES

Child's size 12 jeans or shorts (If you use shorts, you'll need a jeans leg to make the strap.)

1/3 yd. fabric (for lining)

Bias tape (to match lining fabric)

2/3 yd. single-sided fusible ultra-firm fabric stabilizer

Embroidery floss – Red, turquoise, yellow, green

Washable permanent fabric glue (fabric bond)

Red belt

Tracing paper

Transfer paper

TOOLS

Scissors

Sewing machine

Stylus

Pencil

Iron

Fabric marker

Ruler

INSTRUCTIONS

1. Cut 9-1/2" from top of jeans. (Fig. 1)

2. Measure in 1-1/2" on each side. With right sides together, sew seam as shown in Fig. 2 to create straight sides.

3. Trace the embroidery pattern and transfer to front and back pockets. Using three strands of embroidery floss, stem stitch green vine (Photo 1) and satin stitch flower centers and flowers. (Photo 2)

4. Turn jeans inside out. Place bag on ultra firm stabilizer. Using bag (inside out) as pattern, trace around jeans. Cut two from stabilizer.

5. Iron lining fabric on one side of each stabilizer piece. Trim lining fabric even with stabilizer. With lining sides facing, sew side and bottom seams.

6. With jeans turned inside out, sew a 1/4" seam along the bottom edge of the bag. (Fig. 3)

7. Open end corners. Align bottom seam and side seam. Measure 1-1/2" in from each point. Draw a line perpendicular to seam. Sew on line. Repeat for other side. Cut away points, 1/8" from seam. Turn right side out.

8. Repeat step 7 on the lining. Leave lining turned with stabilizer side out.

9. To make the strap, cut a 4" x 30" strip denim from a jeans leg. Fold strip in half lengthwise. Press to crease center. Fold each long raw edge to center. Press. Fold strip in half lengthwise. Press. Topstitch along strap edge.

10. Sew each end inside bag top sides.

11. Finish the top edge of the lining-with-stabilizer with bias tape. Insert lining into jeans bag.

12. Sew or glue lining inside bag along seams and top edge. Let dry.

13. Put belt through belt loops. ❏

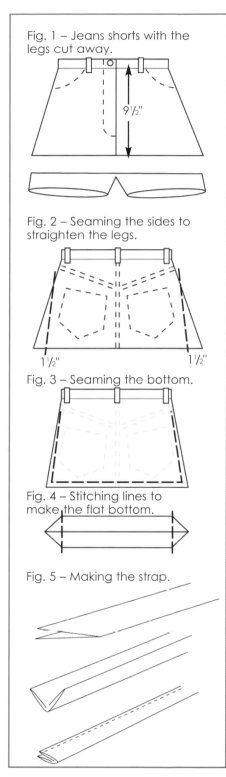

Fig. 1 – Jeans shorts with the legs cut away.

9½"

Fig. 2 – Seaming the sides to straighten the legs.

1½"   1½"

Fig. 3 – Seaming the bottom.

Fig. 4 – Stitching lines to make the flat bottom.

Fig. 5 – Making the strap.

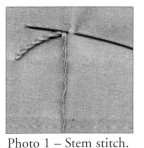

Photo 1 – Stem stitch.

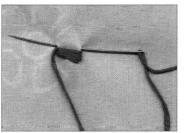

Photo 2 – Satin stitch.

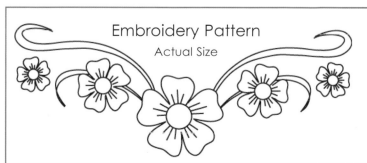

Embroidery Pattern
Actual Size

Touch of the Tropics Tote

Designed by Patty Cox

The round bamboo handles on this tote are held in place by belt loops removed from jeans. It would make a great summer purse or picnic bag. To use as a beach bag, make the lining from waterproof fabric.

SUPPLIES

Jeans

1/2 yd. fabric (for lining)

Single-sided fusible ultra-firm fabric
    stabilizer

8" round bamboo handles

Washable permanent fabric glue
    (fabric bond)

Paper

TOOLS

Scissors

Sewing machine

Iron

Yardstick

Pencil

INSTRUCTIONS

Cut:

1. Cut outside leg seams of jeans, preserv-
   ing inseams. (Fig. 1)
2. Draw a 19" x 14" rectangle on paper.
   Mark 3-1/8" in from each bottom corner. Draw diagonal lines from each
   mark to top corners of pattern. (Fig. 2)
   Cut out paper pattern.
3. Place pattern on denim with jeans
   inseam running diagonally through
   pattern. Cut out denim. (Fig. 3)
4. Turn denim piece upside down on
   jeans, aligning jeans side seam with the
   diagonal line on the pattern. Cut a second denim piece. (Fig. 4)
5. Cut two pieces lining fabric the same
   size. (Fig. 5)
6. Fold paper pattern top down 1". Cut
   two pieces ultra-firm stabilizer. (Fig. 6)
7. Press and fuse each piece of stabilizer to
   the wrong side of the lining fabric.
   Fold the top of the lining fabric over
   the top edge of the stabilizer. Press.
   Repeat for other lining piece.

Sew:

1. With right sides of lining facing, sew
   3/8" seam along both sides and bottom. (Fig. 7)
2. Open bottom seam and align with side
   seams. Draw lines across bottom seam,
   1" in from each end. (Fig. 8) Stitch on
   each line. Trim stabilizer 1/4" from
   each seam. Set aside.
3. With right sides of denim facing, sew
   3/8" seam along both sides and bottom.
   (Fig. 9)
4. Open bottom seam and align with side

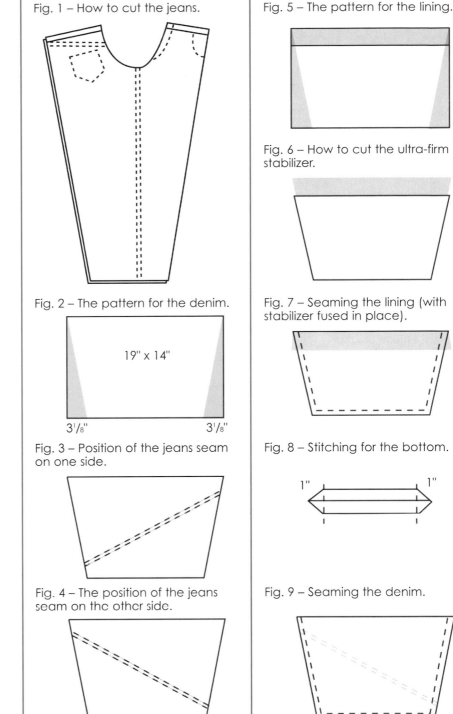

Fig. 1 – How to cut the jeans.

Fig. 2 – The pattern for the denim.

19" x 14"

3¹/₈" 3¹/₈"

Fig. 3 – Position of the jeans seam
on one side.

Fig. 4 – The position of the jeans
seam on the other side.

Fig. 5 – The pattern for the lining.

Fig. 6 – How to cut the ultra-firm
stabilizer.

Fig. 7 – Seaming the lining (with
stabilizer fused in place).

Fig. 8 – Stitching for the bottom.

1" 1"

Fig. 9 – Seaming the denim.

seams. Draw lines across bottom seam, 1" in from each end. Stitch on each line. (Fig. 8)

5. Turn under top raw denim edge 1". Press. Apply a light coat of fabric glue under the
   turned edge.
6. Remove six belt loops from jeans.
7. Position a bamboo handle on one side of tote. Pin the tops of three loops to the tote
   around the handle, using the photo as a guide. Remove bamboo handle. Machine
   stitch top of each belt loop on tote. Reposition bamboo handle on tote. Pin and
   machine stitch the bottom of each belt loop. Repeat for the handle on the other side.
8. Insert lining with stabilizer inside tote. Align bottom corners of stabilized lining with
   inside of tote. Glue or sew top edge of stabilized lining to inside of tote. ❑

Flower Power Tote

A simple rectangular tote bag is decorated with a denim rose and a three-strand beaded tassel. You'll need to use an extra-large pair of jeans in order to cut the tote from one leg. Other options are to use a jeans skirt as the fabric source or to piece the bag.

Designed by Patty Cox

SUPPLIES

Jeans or denim skirt

1/2 yd. fabric (for lining)

Blue upholstery thread

Beads:

    4mm crystal bicones

    8mm amber bicones

    8mm navy faceted round beads

    18mm faceted rectangular beads

    3 faceted drops

Beading thread

1 yd. navy blue webbing, 1" wide

Washable permanent fabric glue

TOOLS

Beading needle

Sewing machine

Scissors

Sewing needle

Iron

INSTRUCTIONS

Cut:

1. Cut two pieces of denim, each 16-1/2" x 18-1/2", with the French seam running down the center of each piece and the hemmed edge at the top. (Fig. 1)

2. Cut two pieces of the lining fabric the same size.

Sew:

1. With right sides of denim pieces facing, sew side and bottom seams.

2. Press open at bottom seam. Align bottom seam and side seam. Measure 1-1/2" in from point. Draw a line perpendicular to seam. (Fig. 2) Sew on line. Repeat for other side. Turn right side out.

3. With right sides of the lining pieces facing, sew side and bottom seams. Press open bottom seam. Align bottom seam and side seam. Measure 1-1/2" in from point. (Fig. 2) Draw a line perpendicular to seam. Sew on line. Repeat for other side. Set aside.

4. For the handles, cut two 18" pieces of webbing.

5. Measure in 4-1/2" from each side of tote. Sew webbing ends inside the top edge of the tote. (Fig. 3)

Make the Beaded Tassel:

Thread beading needle with beading thread. Knot end. Thread needle from the inside of the tote on the center seam to the outside, 1" down from the top. Add beads according to Fig. 4. Thread the needle through the holes of the faceted drop, then back through the beads. Knot thread on tote fabric. Repeat to make three strands. Knot end of thread securely.

Make Denim Rose:

1. Cut a strip of denim 3" x 30". Fold in half lengthwise, right sides together. Sew a seam across each end. Turn right side out.

2. Gather long raw edges together with upholstery thread. Pull gathers tightly. Knot thread securely.

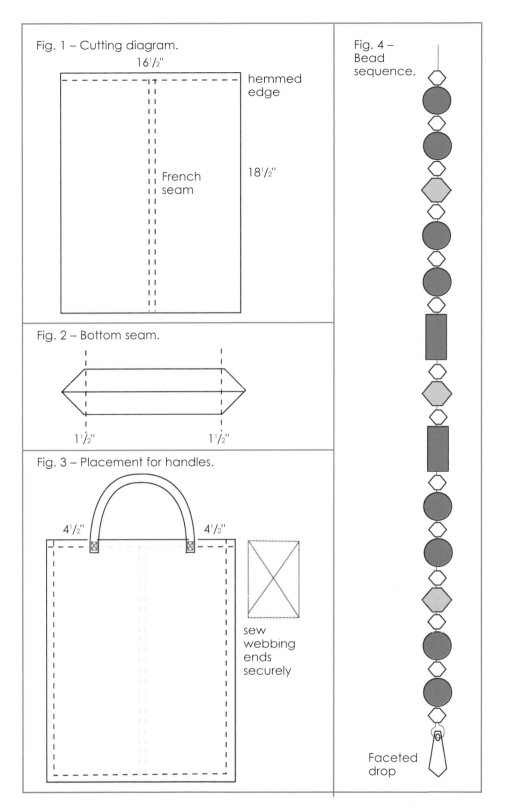

Fig. 1 – Cutting diagram.

16½"

hemmed edge

French seam

18½"

Fig. 2 – Bottom seam.

1½"   1½"

Fig. 3 – Placement for handles.

4½"   4½"

sew webbing ends securely

Fig. 4 – Bead sequence.

Faceted drop

3. Tightly coil gathered strip. Sew gathered edge of coil together. Knot thread securely. Cut thread.

4. Sew or glue rose above the beaded tassel.

Add Lining:

1. Turn under the top raw edge of the lining. Press.

2. Place lining in tote (wrong side of fabric facing out).

3. Stitch turned edge inside tote. ❏

Chenille Sensation Bag

Designed by Patty Cox

A section of a jeans leg, hemmed at the bottom and lined, makes a simple, striking bag with the addition of rounded wooden or plastic handles and a sumptuous chenille fringe.

SUPPLIES

Jeans
1/3 yd. lining fabric
40" chenille fringe
Purse handles, 6-1/4" x 4-1/2"
2 brass D-rings

TOOLS

Sewing machine
Iron

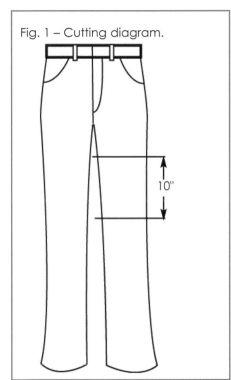

Fig. 1 – Cutting diagram.

10"

INSTRUCTIONS

1. Cut a 10" section from the jeans leg that is 8-1/2" wide at one end (which will be the top) and 11" wide at the other end (which will be the bottom). (Fig. 1)

2. Cut two lining pieces the same height and shape, adding a seam allowance to each side.

3. Turn jeans leg section inside out with the French seam positioned so it runs down the center of the front of the bag. (Fig. 2) Sew a 1/4" bottom seam.

4. Press open bottom seam. Measure 1" in from each point. Draw a line perpendicular to seam. Sew on line. Repeat for other side. (Fig. 2) Turn right side out.

5. Fold top raw edge of denim purse under 1/4". Press.

6. With right sides facing, sew lining side and bottom seams. (Fig. 2)

7. Press open bottom seam. Measure 1" in from one point. Draw a line perpendicular to seam. Sew on line. Repeat for other side. (Fig. 2) Set aside.

8. To make handle loops, cut four 2-1/2" denim squares. Fold in half. (Fig. 3) Crease center. Fold raw edges to center. Press. Fold strip in half lengthwise. Press. Topstitch along open edge. Repeat to make four.

9. Fold a strip over each ring of the purse handles. Position the denim handle loops inside the top edge of the purse. Sew securely to the purse. (Fig. 4) Repeat for all four handle rings.

10. Fold over top raw edge of lining 1/4". Press. Place lining, wrong side out, inside purse. Sew lining inside purse.

11. Position and sew chenille fringe around purse top edge. Add a second layer of chenille fringe for more fullness. ❑

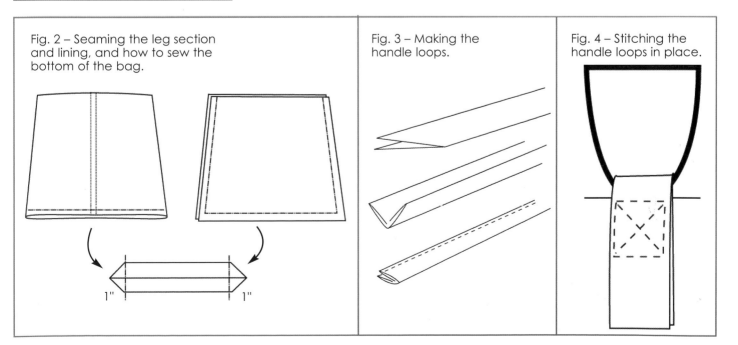

Fig. 2 – Seaming the leg section and lining, and how to sew the bottom of the bag.

1"   1"

Fig. 3 – Making the handle loops.

Fig. 4 – Stitching the handle loops in place.

Both Sides Bag

The design of this bag incorporates both the right front and right back pocket sections from a pair of jeans. We also show how to make your own leather label to decorate and personalize the back pocket side. The bottom of the bag is trimmed with purchased beaded fringe.

Designed by Patty Cox

SUPPLIES

Jeans
1/3 yd. fabric (for lining)
11" beaded fringe
2 D-rings, 1"
Sewing thread
Fabric marker

TOOLS

Scissors
Sewing machine
Measuring tape

Pictured at right: The back pocket side of the bag, complete with a make-your-own printed leather label. The front pocket side of the bag is shown in the photo, *opposite*.

INSTRUCTIONS

1. Align top band of jeans, front and back. Measure down 13". (Fig. 1) Cut left half of jeans front and back at 13". Cut front close to zipper.

2. Open out the cut jeans piece. Place on lining fabric. Cut 1 from lining fabric. Set lining fabric aside.

3. Place beaded fringe upside down on right side of bag lower front. (Fig. 2) Baste in position, using a zipper foot.

4. Fold purse in half, right sides together. Sew 1/4" side seam and bottom seam. (Fig. 3) Turn right side out.

5. For the strap, cut a 4" x 30" strip of denim from a jeans leg. Fold strip in half lengthwise. Press to crease center. (Fig. 4) Fold each raw edge to center. Press. Fold strip in half lengthwise. Press. Topstitch along strap edge.

Continued on page 126

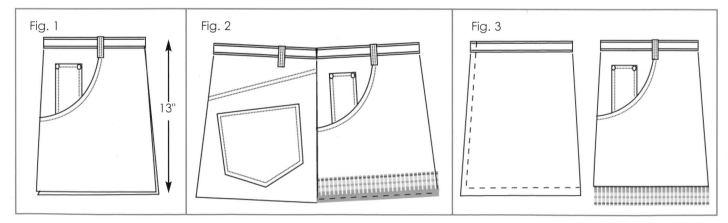

Fig. 1

13"

Fig. 2

Fig. 3

BOTH SIDES BAG

continued from page 124

6. To make the denim strips for the anchor loops for the strap, cut two 4" denim squares from a leg. Fold strip in half. Press to crease center. Fold each raw edge to center. Press. Fold strip in half lengthwise. (Fig. 4) Press. Topstitch along edge.

7. Place one strip through a D-ring. Fold strip in half, aligning raw ends. Place inside jeans waistband at side of bag. Sew tab securely. (Fig. 5) Repeat on other side of bag.

8. Thread one end of the 30" strap through one D-ring. Fold over D-ring 1". Tuck under raw ends of strap. Sew strap end securely. Repeat with other end of strap and other D-ring.

9. Fold lining fabric in half, right sides together. Sew side and bottom seam. Turn top raw edge of lining fabric under 1/4". Press.

10. With wrong side out, place lining in bag. Pin at top. Stitch folded edge of lining to inside of bag, covering the raw ends of the strap anchor loops.

11. *Option:* Sew your own leather label to the waistband above the back pocket. (See the following instructions.) ❑

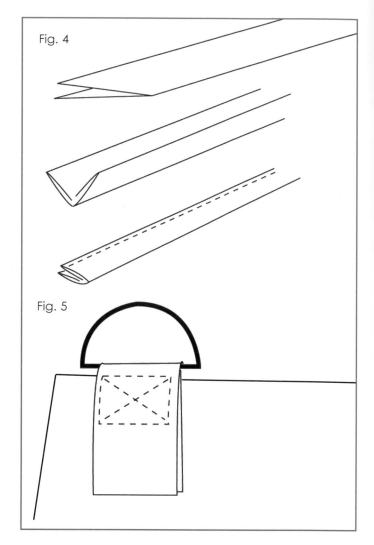

Fig. 4

Fig. 5

Making Your Own Leather Label

You can create your own label design and monogram on your computer. Here's how:

SUPPLIES & TOOLS

Deer skin or thin leather, 3-1/2" x 3"

Computer and printer

Spray adhesive

1 sheet 20-lb. bond paper

INSTRUCTIONS

1. Design a label by drawing one and scanning it or using a copyright-free design on a CD.
2. Print label art on 20-lb. bond paper.
3. Cut a piece of thin deerskin slightly larger than the label art.
4. Apply spray adhesive to back of deerskin. Adhere skin to paper, covering label art.
5. Place paper with deerskin back in printer. Print label art on deerskin.
6. Cut out leather label, leaving the paper backing on the leather.
7. Sew label in position on bag along edges. ❑

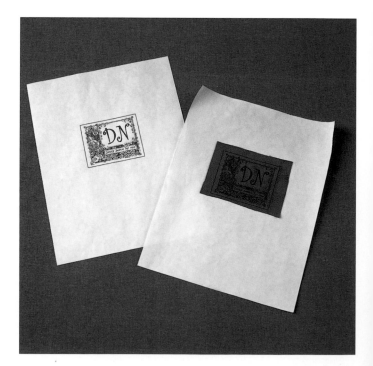

Metric Conversion Chart

Inches to Millimeters and Centimeters

Inches	MM	CM	Inches	MM	CM
1/8	3	.3	2	51	5.1
1/4	6	.6	3	76	7.6
3/8	10	1.0	4	102	10.2
1/2	13	1.3	5	127	12.7
5/8	16	1.6	6	152	15.2
3/4	19	1.9	7	178	17.8
7/8	22	2.2	8	203	20.3
1	25	2.5	9	229	22.9
1-1/4	32	3.2	10	254	25.4
1-1/2	38	3.8	11	279	27.9
1-3/4	44	4.4	12	305	30.5

Yards to Meters

Yards	Meters	Yards	Meters
1/8	.11	3	2.74
1/4	.23	4	3.66
3/8	.34	5	4.57
1/2	.46	6	5.49
5/8	.57	7	6.40
3/4	.69	8	7.32
7/8	.80	9	8.23
1	.91	10	9.14
2	1.83		

Index

Index (Continued)